MONTGOMERY COLLEGE LIBRARY
ROCKVILLE CAMPUS

9780836963489

HOLIDAY SELECTIONS

For READINGS
and RECITATIONS

HOLIDAY SELECTIONS

For READINGS *and* RECITATIONS

SPECIALLY ADAPTED TO CHRISTMAS, NEW YEAR, VALENTINE'S DAY, WASHINGTON'S BIRTHDAY, EASTER, ARBOR DAY, DECORATION DAY, FOURTH OF JULY, AND THANKSGIVING

COMPILED BY

Sara Sigourney Rice

Granger Index Reprint Series

BOOKS FOR LIBRARIES PRESS
FREEPORT, NEW YORK

PN
4305
H7   R 72 11904
R6

1972

First Published 1892
Reprinted 1972

Library of Congress Cataloging in Publication Data

Rice, Sara Sigourney, comp.
　　Holiday selections for readings and recitations.

　　(Granger index reprint series)
　　Reprint of the 1892 ed.
　　1. Recitations.　I. Title.
PN4305.H7R6　1972　　　808.5'4　　　72-39402
ISBN 0-8369-6348-2

PRINTED IN THE UNITED STATES OF AMERICA
BY
NEW WORLD BOOK MANUFACTURING CO., INC.
HALLANDALE, FLORIDA 33009

CONTENTS

CHRISTMAS

		PAGE
At Bethlehem	*Sir Edwin Arnold*	5
At Christmas Time		79
Christmas Chimes, The	*Susan Coolidge*	8
Christmas Day	*Charles Kingsley*	9
Christmas Song	*Edmund Hamilton Sears*	24
Christmas Pictures	*D. B. Williamson*	34
Christmas Eve	*Violet Fuller*	35
Christmas Hymn, A	*Richard Watson Gilder*	36
Christmas Morning	*Dora Greenwell*	39
Christmas Time	*Kate Neely Festellis*	41
Child Angel, The	*Hannah More Kohaus*	44
Christmas Tide	*Eliza Cook*	55
Christmas Tree, The	*Lucy Wheelock*	59
Christkindlein	*Friedrich Ruckert*	60
Christmas Day	*Alice Williams Brotherton*	63
Christmas Carol, A	*S. T. Coleridge*	73
Christmas Bells	*George Lansing Taylor*	87
Early Christmas Morning	*Mary B. Peck*	27
Echoes from Bethlehem		57
Enchanted Oak, The	*O. Herford*	26
First Christmas in New England, The	*Hezekiah Butterworth*	29
Goblins The	*Charles Dickens*	68
Joe's Search for Santa Claus	*Irving Bacheller*	13
Kitty's Christmas Offering		50
Letter to Santa Claus, A	*William O. Stoddard*	81
Old Time Bells, The		48
Reward of the Cheerful Candle, The	*Mary V. Worstell*	37
Santa Claus' Agent	*Hannah More Kohaus*	75
Snow Twins, The	*Rev. P. B. Power*	17
Shepherd-Boy's Carol, The		66
Under the Snow	*Robert Collyer*	31

NEW YEAR

Coasting New Year's Eve		96
Dirge for the Year	*Percy Bysshe Shelley*	97
New Year, The	*Colton*	93
New Year's Chime, A		98
New Year, The	*Violet Fuller*	100
Old Year, The	*Violet Fuller*	95
Old and the New Year, The	*Adelaide Anne Procter*	103
Pet and Her Cat		105
Rejoicing upon the New Year's Coming of Age	*Charles Lamb*	101
Song for the New Year	*Eliza Cook*	91

SAINT VALENTINE'S DAY

Diana's Valentine	*Robert Bridges*	116
It Was a Lass	*Mary E. Wilkins*	115
Lady Mabel	*Alfred Austin*	110
Meg May's Valentine		112
Pierrot's Valentine	*Minnie Buchanan Goodman*	118
St. Valentine's Magic Wand	*William Waterfield*	111
St. Valentine's Day	*Edward Valentine*	113
Valentine's Day	*Charles Lamb*	108
Valentine to a Man of Worth	*Edward A. Church*	114

iii

CONTENTS

WASHINGTON'S BIRTHDAY

		PAGE
Approach of the Presidency, The	George Washington	122
Birthday of Washington, The	Rufus Choate	129
Eulogy on Washington	Robert Treat Paine, Jr.	120
Father of His Country, The	Henry Lee	123
President Washington's Receptions	William Sullivan	127
Washington	Eliza Cook	121
Washington's Kiss		124

EASTER

Back Again	Celia Thaxter	144
Blind Communicant, The	Mary E. Lee	151
Crown, The	Ray Palmer	154
Dream that Came True, The	Jean Ingelow	146
Easter Altar Cloth, The	Julia H. Thayer	137
Flower s Easter Message, The	Emile Poulsson	132
In the Breaking of the Day	Francis L. Mace	145
Legend of the Aspen, A	Bernhard Severin Ingeman	149
Mary at the Sepulchre	Sir Edwin Arnold	133
Miracle of the Roses, The	Robert Southey	140
O Christ, Our King		143
Peace	Julia C. R. Dorr	136

ARBOR DAY

Chestnut-Tree, The	Jane Campbell	168
Garden Scene, A	Marvell	169
Heard Ye o' the Tree of Liberty?	Robert Burns	164
Laurel Seed, The	R. H. Horne	167
Liberty Tree		170
Planting the Oak	Hezekiah Butterworth	166
Spring	Henry David Thoreau	156
Spring	Margaret Veley	159
Three Trees	Charles H. Crandall	157
Tree, The	Jones Very	171
West Wind	Carmen Sylva	163
Wild Flowers	Sarah Doudney	172

DECORATION DAY

Dead Trumpeter, The	T. K. Hervey	177
Dead Volunteer, The	J. W. Barker	178
Dead Comrade, The	Richard Watson Gilder	186
Decoration Day	Jane Campbell	175
Fallen, The	John Vance Cheney	179
His Mother's Song		183
Memorial Day	Z. F. Riley	187
Soldier's Tent, The	Helene Vacaresco	174
Volunteer, The	Elbridge Jefferson Cutler	185

FOURTH OF JULY

Advice to My Country	James Madison	194
Fighting Parson, The	Henry Ames Blood	202
Fight, The	Thomas Dunn English	195
Free America		189
Independence Day, 1798	Royall Tyler	193
National Flag, The	Charles Sumner	192
Our Own Dear Land	J. R. Thome	191
Our Land	King	201
Stars and Stripes, The	Lucretia G. Noble	204

THANKSGIVING DAY

Daisy's Thanksgiving		214
Jericho Bob	Anna Eichberg King	208
Margie's Thanksgiving	E. S. Bumstead	216
Polly's Thanksgiving	A. C. Stoddard	217
Thanksgiving	F. R. Havergal	220
Twilight of Thanksgiving, The	William D. Kelly	222

Holiday Selections
For Readings and Recitations

CHRISTMAS

AT BETHLEHEM.

So many hill-sides, crowned with rugged rocks!
  So many simple shepherds keeping flocks
In many moonlit fields! But, only they—
So lone, so long ago, so far away—
On that one winter's night, at Bethlehem,
To have white Angels singing lauds for them!
They only—hinds wrapped in the he-goat's skin—
To hear Heaven's music, bidding Peace begin!
Only for those, of countless watching eyes,
The " Glory of the Lord " glad to arise;
The skies to blaze with gold and silver light
Of seraphs by strong joy flashed into sight;
The wind, for them, with that strange song to swell,—
By too much happiness incredible,—
That tender Anthem of good times to be,
Then at their dawn—not daylight yet, ah me!
" Peace upon Earth! Good-will!" sung to the strings
Of lutes celestial. Nay, if these things,

Too blessed to believe have seemed, or seem,
Not ours the fault, dear Angels! Prove the dream
Waking and true! Sing once again, and make
Moonlight and starlight sweet for earth's sad sake!
* * * * * *
What was it that ye heard? the wind of Night
Playing in cheating tones with touches light,
Amid the palm-plumes? And ye did not gaze
Heart-startled on the stars (albeit the rays
Of that lone orb shot, sparkling, from the East,
Unseen before) for these, largest and least,
Were fold-lamps, lighted nightly; and ye knew
Far differing in glory in the Night's dark blue
Suddenly lit with rose, and pierced with spike
Of golden spear-beam. Oh, a dream, belike!
Some far-fetched Vision, new to peasant's sleep,
Of Paradise stripped bare!—But, why thus keep
Secrets for them? Yet, wherefore, then,
"Rise, and go up to Bethlehem," and unpen
To wolf and jackal all their hapless fold,
So they might "see these things, which had been told
In Heaven's own Voice?"

                           Why put a marvel by
Because too rich with Hope? Why quite deny
The Heavenly story? High cause had they that
    night
To lift the curtain of Hope's hidden light,
To break decree of silence with Love's cry,
Foreseeing how this Babe, born lowlily,
Should—past dispute, since now achieved is this—
Bring Earth's great gifts of blessing and of bliss.

Wherefore, let whosoever will drink dry
His cup of faith; and think that, verily,
Not in a vision, no way otherwise
Than those poor shepherds told, there did arise
This portent. Being amid their sheep and goats,
Lapped careless in their pasture-keeping coats,
Blind as their drowsy beasts to what drew nigh,
(Such the lulled ear, and such th' unbusied eye
Which ofttimes hears and sees hid things!) there
    spread
The "Glory of the Lord" around each head,
A Light not morn-glow, nor the grey of Night,
Nor lightning-flash, nor lit like any light
By earthly orbs beheld, for Dusk full Noon,
Shining behind the Blue, past Sun and Moon,
Flooding their minds, filling their hearts; around,
Above, below, disclosing grove and ground,
The rocks, the hill, the town, the solitude,
The wondering flocks,— agaze, with grass half-
    chewed,—
The palm-crowns, and the path to Bethlehem,
As sight angelic spies. And, came to them
The "Angel of the Lord," visible, sure,
Known for the Angel by his presence pure
Whereon was written Love, and Peace, and Grace,
With beauty passing mortal mien and face,
Supreme, majestical! for terror fell—
With worship,—on their hearts, the writings tell;
So that the Angel of the Earth had need
To comfort them, speaking these words, indeed:

"Fear not! For behold I bring you Good Tidings
of great joy, which shall be to all people."

"For unto you is born this day in the city of
David, a Saviour, which is Christ the Lord."

"And this the sign unto you! Ye shall find the
babe wrapped in swaddling clothes lying in a manger."

So high, so new, so glad, so comforting,
"Good tidings of great joy to you I bring!"
And so, from Heaven that night th' Evangel fell:
" Beginnings of the Golden Times we tell!
Now is the new Law opened! Mary's son
Hath opened it, and, when full years are run,
Peace shall be, and Good-will, and Mercy shed
Over all flesh and spirit, quick and dead!
The consummation comes, the purposed Bliss;
Earth was for Now; her glad days spring from this!"
SIR EDWIN ARNOLD.

THE CHRISTMAS CHIMES.

THE Christmas chimes are pealing high
   Beneath the solemn Christmas sky,
And blowing winds their notes prolong
Like echoes from an angel's song;
"Good-will and peace, peace and good-will,"
Ring out the carols glad and gay,

Telling the heavenly message still,
  That Christ the Child was born to-day.

In lowly hut and palace hall
Peasant and King keep festival,
And childhood wears a fairer guise,
And tenderer shine all mothers' eyes;
The aged man forgets his years,
  The mirthful heart is doubly gay,
The sad are cheated of their tears,
  For Christ the Lord was born to-day.
                              SUSAN COOLIDGE.

CHRISTMAS DAY.

How will it dawn, the coming Christmas Day?
  A Northern Christmas, such as painters love,
And kinsfolk, shaking hands but once a year;
And dames who tell old legends by the fire?
Red sun, blue sky, white snow, and pearléd ice,
Keen, stinging air, which sets the blood on fire,
And makes the old man merry with the young,
Through the short sunshine, through the longer
    night?
Or Southern Christmas, dark and dank with mist,
And heavy with the scent of steaming leaves,
And rosebuds moldering on the dripping porch;
One twilight, without rise or set of sun;
Till beetles drone along the hollow lane,
And round the leafless hawthorns flitting bats

Hawk the pale moths of winter? Welcome, then,
At best, the flying gleam, the flying shower,
The rain-pools glittering on the long white roads,
And shadows sweeping on from down to down
Before the salt Atlantic gale: yet come
In whatsoever garb, or sad, or gay,
Come fair, come foul, 'twill still be Christmas Day.

How will it dawn, the coming Christmas Day?
To sailors, lounging on the lonely deck
Beneath the rushing trade-winds? Or to him,
Who, by some noisome harbor of the East,
Watches swart arms roll down the precious bales,
Spoils of the tropic forests; year by year,
Amid the din of heathen voices, groaning,
Himself half heathen? How to those brave hearts
Who toil with laden loins and sinking stride,
Beside the bitter wells of treeless sands,
Toward the peaks which flood the ancient Nile,
To free a tyrant's captors? How to those—
New patriarchs of the new-founded underworld,
And count their flocks' increase? To them that day
Shall dawn in glory, and solstitial blaze
Of full midsummer sun; to them that mourn,
Gay flowers beneath their feet, gay birds aloft,
Shall tell of naught but summer; but to them,
Ere yet, unwarned by carol or by chime,
They spring into the saddle, thrills may come
From that great heart of Christendom which beats
Round all the worlds: and gracious thoughts of
      youth;

Of steadfast folk who worship God at home;
Of wise words learnt beside their mother's knee;
Of innocent faces upturned once again
In awe and joy to listen to the tale
Of God made man, and in a manger laid;
May soften, purify, and raise the soul
From selfish cares, and growing lust of gains,
And phantoms of this dream which some call life,
Toward the eternal facts; for, here or there,
Summer or winter, 'twill be Christmas Day.

Blest day, which aye reminds us, year by year,
What 'tis to be a man; to curb and spurn
The tyrant in us; that ignoble self
Which boasts, not loathes, its likeness to a beast,
And owns no good save ease, no ill save pain,
No purpose, save its share in that wild war,
In which, through countless ages, living things
Compete in internecine greed.   Oh, God!
Are we as creeping things, which have no Lord?
That we are brutes, great God, we know too well:
Apes dainty-featured; silly birds, who flaunt
Their plumes unheeding of the fowler's steps;
Spiders, who catch with paper, not with nets;
Tigers, who slay with cannon and sharp steel,
Instead of teeth and claws—all these we are.
Are we not more than these, save in degree?
No more than these; and born but to compete—
To envy and devour, like beast or herd;
Mere fools of Nature; puppets of strong lusts;
Taking the sword, to perish with the sword,
Upon the universal battle-field,

Even as the things upon the moor outside?
The heath eats up green grass and delicate flowers,
The pine eats up the heath, the grub the pine,
The finch the grub, the hawk the silly finch;
And man, the mightiest of all beasts of prey,
Eats what he lists; the strong eats up the weak;
The many eat the few, great nations small;
And he who cometh in the name of all—
He greediest triumphs by the greed of all;
And, armed by his own victims, eats up all;
While ever out of the eternal heavens
Looks patient down the great, magnanimous God,
Who, Maker of all worlds, did sacrifice
All to Himself! Nay, but Himself to One!
Who taught mankind on that first Christmas Day
What 'twas to be a man: to give, not take;
To serve, not rule; to nourish, not devour;
To help, not crush; if need, to die, not live!

Oh! blessed Day, which gives the eternal lie
To self, and sense, and all the brute within;
Oh! come to us amid this war of life;
To hall and hovel, come; to all who toil
In senate, shop, or study; and to those
Who, sundered by the wastes of half a world,
Ill-warned, and sorely tempted, ever face
Nature's brute powers, and men unmanned to brutes.
Come to them, blest and blessing, Christmas Day;
Tell them once more the tale of Bethlehem—
The kneeling shepherds, and the Babe Divine;
And keep them men, indeed, fair Christmas Day.
CHARLES KINGSLEY.

JOE'S SEARCH FOR SANTA CLAUS.

A STORY, my child? Well, there's none that I
know
As good as the story about little Joe.
He lived with his mother, just under the eaves
Of a tenement high, where the telegraph weaves
Its highway of wire, that everywhere goes,
And makes the night musical when the wind blows.
Their home had no father—the two were bereft
Of all but their appetites—those never left!
Joe's grew with his thought; a day never passed
He spent not in hunger to make the food last;
And days when his mother silently went
And stood by the windows—Joe knew what it meant.
They'd nothing for supper! The words were so sad
That somehow they drowned all the hunger he had.
And surely God's miracles never have ceased—
Joe's hunger grew less when his sorrows increased.

When the coal ran out in winter's worst storm,
The fire burnt the harder that kept their hearts warm.
Their windows revealed many wonderful sights,
Long acres of roofing and high-flying kites;
At sunset, the great vault of heaven aglow,
The lining of gold on the clouds hanging low,
The cross on the top of St. Mary's high tower
Ablaze with the light of that magical hour;
And still, as the arrows of light slanted higher,
The last thing in sight was the great cross of fire.

Each day, as it vanished, the history old
Of Christ's crucifixion was reverently told,
To Him the boy learned to confide all his woes,
But oftenest prayed for a new suit of clothes,
Since those that he wore didn't fit him at all—
The coat was too large and the trousers too small,
And Joe looked so queer, from his head to his feet,
It grieved his proud soul to be seen in the street.
And sometimes he cherished a secret desire
To own a hand-sled, or to build a bonfire;
But reached one conclusion by various routes—
He could have better fun with a new pair of boots.
He thought how the old pair, when shiny and whole
Had squeaked in a way that delighted his soul,
And remembrance grew sad as he strutted around
And tried hard, but vainly, to waken that sound.
The day before Christmas brought trouble to Joe,
A thousand times worse.   'Twas a terrible blow
To hear that old Santa Claus, god of his dreams,
Would not come that year with his fleet-footed teams.
He'd seen them.   Why, once, of a night's witching
    hour
He saw them jump over the cross on the tower
And scamper away o'er the snow-covered roofs,
His heart beating time to the sound of their hoofs.
Not coming this year?   Santa Claus must be dead,
He thought, as with sad tears he crept into bed.
And, as he lay thinking, the long strings of wire
Sang low in the wind like a deep-sounding lyre,
And Joe caught the notes of this solemn refrain—
"He'll not come again! no, he'll not come again!"

And oh! how the depths of his spirit were stirred
By thoughts that were born of the music he heard!
How cold were the winds, and they sang, in their
  strife,
Of storms yet to come in the winters of life.
They mocked him, but mark how the faith of the
  child
Stood firm as a fortress, its hope undefiled;
For still the boy thought that, if Santa Claus knew
How great were their needs and their comforts how
  few,
He would come; and at length, when the first rays
  of light
Had fathomed the infinite depths of the night,
And brightened the windows, Joe cautiously crept
Out of bed; and he dressed while his mother still
  slept,
And down the long stairways on tiptoe he ran;
Then out in the snow, with the will of a man,
He went, looking hither and thither, because,
Poor boy! he was trying to find Santa Claus.

  He hurried along through the snow-burdened street
As if the good angels were guiding his feet;
And as the sun rose in the heavens apace,
A radiance fell on his uplifted face
That came from the cross gleaming far overhead—
A symbol of hope for the living and dead.
A moment he looked at the great house of prayer,
Then shyly peeked in to see what was there;
And entering softly he wandered at will
Through pathways of velvet, deserted and still,

And saw the light grow on a wonderful scene
Of ivy-twined columns and arches of green,
And back of the rail, where the clergyman knelt,
He sat on the cushions to see how they felt.
How soft was that velvet he stroked with his hand !
But when he lay down, oh, the feeling was grand!
And while he was musing the walls seemed to sway,
And slowly the windows went moving away.
What, ho! there he comes! with his big pack and all.
Down the sunbeams that slope from the high-win-
    dowed wall ;
And Joe tried to speak, but could not, if he died,
When Santa Claus came and sat down by his side.
"A tenement boy! humph! he probably swears."
(Joe trembled, and tried hard to think of his prayers.)
He lifted Joe's eyelids, he patted his brow,
And said, " He is not a bad boy, anyhow."
But hark! there is music ; a deep-swelling sound
Is sweeping on high as if heavenward bound.
And suddenly waking, Joe saw kneeling there
The rector, long-robed, who was reading a prayer.
" Provide for the fatherless children," said he,
" The widowed, the helpless, the bond and the free."
The rector stops praying—his face wears a frown ;
A ragged young gamin is pulling his gown.
"I knowed you would come," said the boy, half in
    fright—
"I knowed you would come—I was watchin' all
    night.
Say! what are ye goin' t' give mother an' me?
Le'me see what 'tis, Santa Claus—please le'me see!"

The rector looked down into Joe's honest face,
And a great wave of feeling swept over the place;
And tenderly laying his hand on Joe's head,
He turned to the people and solemnly said:
" We pray that the poor may be sheltered and fed,
And we leave it to Heaven to furnish the bread.
Ye know, while He feedeth the fowls of the air,
The children of mankind He leaves to man's care;"
And kissing Joe's face the preacher said then:
" Of such is the kingdom of Heaven. Amen!"
That day Santa Claus came to many a door
He'd forgotten to call at the evening before.
Was little Joe lucky? Well, now, you are right,
And the wires sang merrily all the next night.
IRVING BACHELLER

THE SNOW TWINS.

JOHN UMPH knew it was Christmas-time, and he knew people ate roast-beef and plum-pudding. He knew, also, there was none for him; but he did not seem very much to mind. He was almost always more or less under the influence of the sleeping draught, which was supplied to him from the neighboring hospital, to kill the pain.

But his two little ones—Toby and Kitty—had all their wits about them, and at the present moment these wits were being exercised about keeping Christmas, especially with reference to their father. After much consultation, they determined they would go out on Christmas Eve and try whether they could get a few pence by singing carols near some of the great houses—even a few pence would get something for poor father; of themselves they did not think. A couple of pennyworth of lollipops did cross their minds, but in such a fleeting way it was not worthy of being chronicled. But what carols should they sing? The thought must have come to an untimely end had it not been they had a friend outside the court.

Tom Elps did what little good he could; and amongst his small deeds were little kindnesses to the children Umphs. Now, Tom's great solace in life was poetry—or rhymes. He read poetry, and he made—well, whatever you choose to call it. Just now, to be in season, Tom Elps had been carol-making, so the twins Umph were just in the nick of time to get their wants supplied.

Tom quite approved of the twins Umph going to sing carols, provided they did not go too far from home and get lost, and he read out several of his latest compositions from which to choose. The choice finally rested between two:

" One day the angels went a-singing;
   Said they, 'Good news to-day we're bringing.
   Set all the church-bells ding, dong, ringing;
   Jesus Christ is born to-day,
   He's come awhile on earth to stay;
   So all you bells your loudest play:
       Ding, dong, ringing.' "

The other which was chosen was shorter, and easier to sing, ran thus:

> "Jesus Christ is very good:
> He came on Christmas Day;
> And Jesus said He never would
> Drive any one away.
> Up and down,
> Through the town,
> Let every bell
> The story tell,
> That Jesus said He never would
> Drive any one away."

The Umph twins were quick enough at learning such things as they had the chance of, and they were soon fitted with both words and tune. And out of that carol they fondly hoped there would be a good Christmas dinner for their father; and, though they would not allow the idea, still that deceiver and flatterer, Hope, whispered, "And perhaps lollipops for themselves."

It is a peculiarity of the great gulf in Londontown that, though there is, in one sense, a tremendous distance between the top and the bottom of it, in another sense these two extremes are very near each other; hence, we need not be surprised that not far from where Mr. Startcomb lived, at the top of the gulf, in the sunshine and fresh air, lived John Umph, cobbler, down at the bottom, in air close and stifling.

It was therefore no great venture on the part of the Umph twins to present themselves at dark before Mr. Startcomb's hall-door; not only before the door but it will scarcely be credited even on the steps under the portico itself. Mr. Startcomb's house had an advantage above that of his neighbor's, in that it had quite a little garden; moreover, in that garden stood a great tree, and that tree stood right opposite Mr. Startcomb's bedroom window.

Having sung in vain before three or four other houses, the twins Umph now started their carol at Mr. Startcomb's hall-door. Presently the thick curtain which covered the plate-glass therein was cautiously drawn aside a little bit in the centre, and four bright eyes peeped through. They belonged to the Startcomb twins, who were playing in the hall at the time. Then they were drawn open a little more and the twins at the top of the gulf were within an inch of the twins at the bottom of the gulf, only, as of course there ought to be, there was nearly half an inch of plate-glass between them. But you see that half-inch made all the difference—at the Startcomb side was a bright fire in the hall, and carpet and light; at the Umph side were darkness and uncovered stone and bitter cold.

The Startcomb children could hear the words of the carol quite distinctly:

> "Jesus Christ is very good,
>   He came on Christmas Day,
> And Jesus said He never would
>   Drive any one away."

Oh, that it were Christmas Day! They should
give their money—something to give; for the brilliant
light from the hall showed the two little faces outside
were wan and pale and thin. But the Startcomb twins
would run to their father and say the carol to him.
He had plenty of new money. This they knew, for
he had jingled a bag of it before them, and told them
their Christmas boxes were inside. Perhaps he
wouldn't mind giving them a little bit before—on
Christmas Eve.

They found their father before the study-fire, and
rushed in to him as children will rush, and repeated
the carol to him, and begged for the Christmas box
now, that they might have something to give; but
Mr. Startcomb was furious.

"The impudent brats," said Mr. Startcomb to his
children; "I'll soon make them go," and he was
jumping up for the purpose when he was caught by
each leg by one of the children. They kept saying

"And Jesus said He never would
Drive any one away."

"Well, if Jesus wouldn't, I will." But he had at
last to give in, and he pulled three penny pieces out
of his pocket. "Begone!" said Mr. Startcomb as he
gave the Umphs the money, "and never come back
here as long as you're alive. If you do, I'll give you
to the police."

With that the angry man slammed the door, but
not before the twin Umphs had perceived the twins

Startcomb had bestowed upon them sundry nods and smiles. Enriched with which as much as with the money the twins Umph descended the portico steps, but not to go away at once, only as far as the big tree under which they stationed themselves, hoping by some happy chance they might again see the happy faces which had given them kind looks on that to them cheerless Christmas Eve. They intended to remain just a few minutes, then make for what they called "home," and see what they could get to make father a Christmas feast.

There stood the twins Umph close together, with their backs to the tree, not knowing the meaning of "minutes," when spent in biting cold, to those who are ill-shod, ill-clad, and whose systems are enfeebled by long want of proper food. A treacherous slumber soon began to steal over the weary children. They slept as they stood, leaning backward on and supported by the great tree; and as they slept, the blood crept more and more slowly through their veins.

Mr. Startcomb had not slept well that Christmas Eve. Somehow he was haunted with that terrible thing which he had said, that he would do what Jesus would not. He had told those two children never to come back to his house as long as they were alive; but what if they should come back when they were dead? Pooh! pooh! Who ever heard of such a thing? That might do for a ghost story; but he was a man of the world, and did not believe in ghosts, and so Mr. Startcomb fell into a troubled sleep. But it was not for very long. After dozing and waking on and off until about two in the morning, he got up and drew the blind and looked out. Oh! horror! There, under the tree, leaning against it, were two white objects, the outlines certainly of children, and of the same size as those he had told never to come back to him alive. Could these be those children? And, if so, whence had they come? Why were they that shape? Why were they so white? The horror-struck man staggered back to his bed and covered his head with his bed-clothes, and lay shaking there until morning came. Then when the servant came he found his master partially paralyzed.

Ere long, the gardener, going along the path, saw the white figures standing, as it were, under the tree, and, going up to them and seeing they were snow-covered human beings, called the police. An inquest was held, and a verdict was returned—"Died of exposure"—and much perplexity was caused by the fact that each of the children held an old, worn three-penny piece. Mr. Startcomb had grudged them even a new one; as he must give, he had given the worst he had.

When the little Umphs went forth to sing their carol, their poor father was in worse pain than usual, and, by way of easing it, he ventured on double the portion of his sleeping draught. This was too much for him, and he never woke from the sleep it produced.

Many Christmas Eves have come and gone since that eventful one, and Startcomb's house now keeps festival in a very different way from that of old. On

Christmas Eve great preparations are made, and on Christmas night what they are made for comes to pass.

Then may you see a young man and young woman feasting in the Startcomb kitchen as many children as it will hold; every child receives a new three-penny piece and a half-crown besides. Time has softened for Richard and Mary Startcomb the sad features of the long-past dreadful Christmas Eve. Year by year they commemorate the children's death, and, better still, day by day, they try even more and more to live as lived One whose carol was sung at their door.

REV. P. B. POWER.

CHRISTMAS SONG.

CALM on the listening ear of night
   Come Heaven's melodious strains,
Where wild Judea stretches far
   Her silver-mantled plains;
Celestial choirs from courts above
   Shed sacred glories there;
And angels with their sparkling lyres
   Make music on the air.

The answering hills of Palestine
   Send back the glad reply,
And greet from all their holy heights
   The day-spring from on high:

O'er the blue depths of Galilee
   There comes a holier calm,
And Sharon waves, in solemn praise
   Her silent groves of palm.

"Glory to God!" The lofty strain
   The realm of ether fills:
How sweeps the song of solemn joy
   O'er Judah's sacred hills!
"Glory to God!" The sounding skies
   Loud with their anthems ring:
"Peace on the earth; good-will to men,
   From Heaven's eternal King!"

Light on thy hills, Jerusalem!
   The Saviour now is born:
More bright on Bethlehem's joyous plains
   Breaks the first Christmas morn;
And brighter on Moriah's brow,
   Crowned with her temple-spires,
Which first proclaim the new-born light,
   Clothed with its Orient fires.

This day shall Christian lips be mute,
   And Christian hearts be cold?
Oh, catch the anthem that from Heaven
   O'er Judah's mountains rolled!
When nightly burst from seraph-harps
   The high and solemn lay,—
"Glory to God! on earth be peace;
   Salvation comes to-day!"
                EDMUND HAMILTON SEARS.

THE ENCHANTED OAK.

BENEATHE an ancient oake one daye
   A holye friar kneeled to praye.
Scarce hadde he mumbled Aves three
When lo! a voice within the tree
Straighte to the friar's hearte it wente.
A voice as of some spirit pente
Within the hollow of the tree
That cried, " Good father, sette me free."

Quothe he, " This hath an evil sounde,"
Ande bent him lower to the grounde.
But ever tho' he prayed, the more
The voice hys pytie didde implore,
Untyl he raised hys eyes ande there
Behelde a mayden ghostlie faire.
Thus to the holye manne she spoke:

" Within the hollowe of this oake
   Enchanted for a hundred yeares,
   Have I been bounde—yette vain my teares!
Notte anything can breake the banne
Till I be kissed by holye manne."

" Woe's me," thenne sayd the friar, " if thou
   Be sente to tempt me breake my vowe.
   Butte whether mayde or fiende thou be,
I'll stake my soul to sette thee free."

The holye manne then crossed hym thrice
And kissed the mayde—when in a trice
She vanished.
   "Heaven forgive me now,"
Exclaimed the friar. "my broken vowe."

"If I have sinned, I sinned to save
Another fromme a living grave."
Thenne downe upon the earth he felle,
And prayed some sign that he might telle
If he were doomed evermore;
When lo! the oake alle bare before
Put forth a branch of palest greene,
And fruited everywhere betweene,
With waxen berries, pearlie white,
A miracle before hys sight.
* * * * *
The holye friar wente hys waye
And told hys tale.
   And from thatte daye
It hath been writ that anye manne
May blamelesse kiss what mayde he canne;
Nor any one shall say hym "no"
Beneathe the holye mistletoe.
O. HERFORD.

EARLY CHRISTMAS MORNING.

FOUR little feet pattering on the floor,
 Two tangled curly heads peeping at the door,
Hear the merry laughter, happy, childish roar,
  Early Christmas morning.

Two little stockings full of sweets and toys,
Everything charming for little girls and boys.
How could they help, then, making such a noise,
    Early Christmas morning?

Down beside the stockings many gifts were spread,
Dollies, drums, a cradle, and a brand new sled.
"Haven't we too many?" little Nellie said
    Early Christmas morning.

Four little bare feet on the sidewalk cold,
Two little faces with want and hunger old
Peeping through the window where those gifts unrolled,
    Early Christmas morning.

"Yes," says John to Nellie, as he spied the two.
"We've so many presents, tell you what we'll do.
I'll give half of mine away. Now, dear Nell will you?"
    Early Christmas morning.

Two little famished ones into the house were called,
Favors heaped upon them till they stood enthralled
Was not this the angel's song, "Peace, good-will to all!"
    Early Christmas morning?

MARY B. PECK.

THE FIRST CHRISTMAS IN NEW ENGLAND

THEY thought they had come to their port that day,
   But not yet was their journey done;
And they drifted away from Provincetown Bay
   In the fireless light of the sun.
With rain and sleet were the tall masts iced,
   And gloomy and chill was the air,
But they looked from the crystal sails to Christ,
   And they came to a harbor fair.
      The white hills silent lay,—
        For there were no ancient bells to ring,
        No priests to chant, no choirs to sing,
        No chapel of baron, or lord, or king,
          That gray, cold winter day.

The snow came down on the vacant seas,
   And white on the lone rocks lay,—
But rang the axe 'mong the evergreen trees
   And followed the Sabbath day.
Then rose the sun in a crimson haze,
   And the workmen said at dawn:
"Shall our axes swing on this day of days,
   When the Lord of life was born?"
      The white hills silent lay,—
        For there were no ancient bells to ring,
        No priests to chant, no choirs to sing,
        No chapel of baron, or lord, or king,
          That gray, cold Christmas Day

" The old town's bells we seem to hear:
   They are ringing sweet on the Dee;
They are ringing sweet on the Harlem Meer,
   And sweet on the Zuyder Zee.
The pines are frosted with snow and sleet.
   Shall we our axes wield
When the chimes at Lincoln are ringing sweet
   And the bells of Austerfield?"
         The air was cold and gray,—
            And there were no ancient bells to ring,
            No priests to chant, no choirs to sing,
            No chapel of baron, or lord, or king,
               That gray, cold Christmas Day.

Then the master said, " Your axes wield,
   Remember ye Malabarre Bay;
And the covenant there with the Lord ye sealed
   Let your axes ring to-day.
You may talk of the old town's bells to-night.
   When your work for the Lord is done,
And your boats return, and the shallop's light
   Shall follow the light of the sun.
         The sky is cold and gray,—
            And here are no ancient bells to ring,
            No priests to chant, no choirs to sing,
            No chapel of baron, or lord, or king,
               This gray, cold Christmas Day.

" If Christ was born on Christmas Day,
   And the day by Him is blest,
Then low at His feet the evergreens lay
   And cradle His church in the West.

Immanuel waits at the temple gates
  Of the nation to-day ye found,
And the Lord delights in no formal rites,
  To-day let your axes sound!"
      The sky was cold and gray,—
      And there were no ancient bells to ring,
      No priests to chant, no choirs to sing,
      No chapel of baron, or lord, or king,
          That gray, cold Christmas Day.

Their axes rang through the evergreen trees
  Like the bells on the Thames and Tay;
And they cheerily sung by the windy seas,
  And they thought of Malabarre Bay.
On the lonely heights of Burial Hill
  The old Precisioners sleep;
But did ever men with a nobler will
  A holier Christmas keep,
      When the sky was cold and gray,—
      And there were no ancient bells to ring,
      No priests to chant, no choirs to sing,
      No chapel of baron, or lord, or king,
          That gray, cold Christmas Day?
              HEZEKIAH BUTTERWORTH.

UNDER THE SNOW.

IT was Christmas Eve in the year fourteen.
  And, as ancient dalesmen used to tell,
The wildest winter they ever had seen.
  With the snow lying deep on moor and fell.

When Wagoner John got out his team,
  Smiler and Whitefoot, Duke and Gray,
With the light in his eyes of a young man's dream,
  As he thought of his wedding on New Year's Day

To Ruth, the maid with the bonnie brown hair,
  And eyes of the deepest, sunniest blue,
Modest and winsome, and wondrous fair,
  And true to her troth, for her heart was true.

" Thou's surely not going!" shouted mine host;
  " Thou'll be lost in the drift, as sure as thou's born;
Thy lass winnot to be wed wi' a ghost,
  And that's what thou'll be on Christmas morn.

" It's eleven long miles from Skipton toon
  To Blueberg hooses 'e Washburn dale:
Thou had better turn back and sit thee doon,
  And comfort thy heart wi' a drop o' good ale."

But what cares the lover for storm or drift,
  Or peril of death on the haggard way?
He sings to himself like a lark in the lift,
  And the joy in his heart turns December to May.

But the wind from the north brings a deadly chill
  Creeping into his heart, and the drifts are deep,
Where the thick of the storm strikes Blueberg Hill.
  He is weary, and falls in a pleasant sleep,

And dreams he is walking by Washburn side,
  Walking with Ruth on a summer's day,

Singing that song to his bonnie bride,
  His own wife now forever and aye.

Now read me this riddle, how Ruth should hear
  That song of a heart in the clutch of doom
Steal on her ear, distinct and clear,
  As if her lover was in the room.

And read me this riddle, how Ruth should know,
  As she bounds to throw open the heavy door,
That her lover was lost in the drifting snow,
  Dying or dead, on the great wild moor.

"Help! help!" "Lost! lost!"
  Rings through the night as she rushes away,
Stumbling, blinded, and tempest-tossed,
  Straight to the drift where her lover lay.

And swift they leap after into the night,
  Into the drifts by Blueberg Hill,
Ridsdale and Robinson, each with a light,
  To find her there holding him white and still.

"Nay, nay, they were wed!" the dalesman cried,
  "By Parson Carmalt o' New Year's Day;
Bless ye! Ruth were me great-great grandsire's bride,
  And Maister Frankland gave her away."

"But how did she find him under the snow?"
  They cried, with a laughter touched with tears.
"Nay, lads," he said, softly, "we never can know—
  No, not if we live a hundred years."

ROBERT COLLYER.

CHRISTMAS PICTURES.

THESE are the merry hours they say,
   The loveliest ones that come and go
And gild our lives with colors gay
   As those which in the blossoms glow,
     Whose skies to happy eyes are bright
     With Peace, and Joy, and Love's own light.

I see the boys, all smiles and glee
   Bear by the green and fragrant pine,
But there are those whose cheeks are wan, ah! me,
   While theirs are ruddy as the wine,
     And their young hearts have had no share
     In Life's great woes, and sad despair.

I hear the swift sleigh's tinkling bell,
   The ringing laugh upon the road,
And see the boys come down the dell
   Beneath their bending holly load,
     For this is Christmas Day for all,
     In cottage low, or princely hall.

And there is gladness everywhere
   This day of all that have been or to be,
It swells along the frosty air,
   From old and young in merry glee,
     And earth and sky seem bright and gay
     Upon this happy Christmas Day.

Charity walks to-day abroad
  With open hands the poor to cheer,
And thankful hearts are blessing God
  That His kind care doth thus appear,
    When cold blasts shriek and storm-clouds lour,
    To brighten thus life's winter-hour.

Oh! happiest day of all the year,
  This long, long wished-for Christmas Day,
List, list, the peal of bells we hear,
  They drive all sorrow far away.
    Father above, let all receive
    The cheer Thy love alone can give.
                              D. B. WILLIAMSON

CHRISTMAS EVE.

THE pure white snow is falling fast,
  O'er hill and dale, o'er tower and town,
The wind is high, a rushing blast,
  And swiftly Christmas Eve comes down.

Oh! happy time! what visions bright
  Around the family hearth now shine;
All hearts are filled with calm delight
  On this sweet eve, this hour divine.

Around the glowing fire they meet—
  The young and old, the brave and fair;
The blushing maid her love doth greet,
  With holly in her shining hair.

The aged grandsire fondly smiles
   On children's children at his knee,
Each pretty word his thought beguiles,
   From days he never more may see;

From vanish'd friends, who, long ago,
   With him did keep the Christmas time,
Who lie within a shroud of snow,
   And covered by the frost and rime.

From them the wanderers far away,
   On land or on the heaving deep,
Who, looking upwards, long for day,
   And turn aside, perchance, to weep.

Alas! that any should be sad
   This holy hour, when Christ was born!
Shine, light of God, and make us glad,
   And quickly rise, fair Christmas morn!
                          VIOLET FULLER.

A CHRISTMAS HYMN.

TELL me what is this innumerable throng
   Singing in the heavens a loud angelic song?
These are they who come with swift and shining feet
From round about the throne of God the Lord of Light to greet.

Oh, who are these that hasten beneath the starry
    sky—
As if with joyful tidings that through the world shall
    fly?—
The faithful shepherds these, who greatly were
    afeared
When as they watched their flocks by night, the
    heavenly host appeared.

Who are these that follow across the hills of night
A star that westward hurries along the fields of light?
Three wise men from the East who myrrh and treas-
    ure bring
To lay them at the feet of Him, their Lord, and Christ,
    and King.

What babe new-born is this that in a manger cries?
Near on her lowly bed his happy mother lies.
Oh, see the air is shaken with white and heavenly
    wings—
This is the Lord of all the earth, this is the King of
    kings!

RICHARD WATSON GILDER.

THE REWARD OF THE CHEERFUL CANDLE.

ONCE upon a time two little candles lay side by
side in a big box. Both were pure white.

Said one, "I wonder what will become of us? Do
you think we could be meant for a Christmas tree?"

(For you must know that to be put on a Christmas tree is the best possible thing that can happen to a candle.)

"Of course not!" said the other, who was cross. "If we are meant for a Christmas tree it will be for some shabby little children, see if it isn't."

"If we are," said the first, "I'll shine my very brightest; for the eyes of even poor children, with only few pleasures in prospect, are enough to rival little candles on Christmas Eve."

"If we are," grumbled the second, "I am not sure that I will allow myself to be lighted at all."

Christmas Eve drew nearer and nearer. Sure enough, the two little candles, with many others of blue and pink and yellow and red, were bought for a Christmas tree.

On the day before Christmas, while it still was daylight, some young girls came to arrange the presents, and make the tree ready for the evening.

"Oh! what a lot of pretty little candles!" said one of them. "They are such lovely colors—all except those two white ones. We will put those out of sight, because the red and pink ones are prettier."

"Didn't I tell you what would happen?" said the cross little candle, in a whisper.

"Yes; but wait," replied the other. "Just shine your brightest all the time."

"I won't!" snapped the cross one.

When evening came, ranged all round the tree were happy boys and girls. Soon every bough on the great tree blossomed with little lights. Some of

the flames were faint, but many were bright. When
the little white candles were lighted, the cross one
just sputtered a minute, and then went out. The
other shone so brightly that a gentleman standing
near said:

"Oh! what a brilliant little candle—but it is almost out of sight among the green branches. We
ought to put it where it can be seen better."

"Put it on the very tip-top," said a little lady.

And that is where they did put it—on the very
tip-top of the tree, where it nodded and gleamed in
answer to the smiling faces all around it.

MARY V. WORSTELL.

CHRISTMAS MORNING

"GOOD Christians rise, this is the morn
   When Christ the Saviour, He was born,
All in a stable so lowly,
At Bethlehem in Galilee.
Rejoice! our Saviour, He was born,
On Christmas Day in the morning."

   *   *   *   *   *

If ye would hear the angels sing,
  "Peace on earth and mercy mild."
   Think of Him who was once a child,
On Christmas Day in the morning.

If you would hear the angels sing,
  Christians, see ye let each door

Stand wider than ever it stood before,
On Christmas Day in the morning.

Rise and open wide the door,
    Christians, rise! the world is wide,
    And many there be that stand outside,
Yet Christmas comes in the morning.

If ye would hear the angels sing,
    Rise and spread your Christmas fare,
    'Tis merrier still the more that share,
On Christmas Day in the morning.

If ye would hear the angels sing,
    Rise, and light your Christmas fires
    And see that ye pile the logs still higher,
On Christmas Day in the morning.

Rise and light your Christmas fires,
    Christians, rise! the world is old
    And time is weary and worn and cold,
Yet Christmas comes in the morning.

If ye would hear the angels sing,
    Rise and spice your wassail bowl
    With warmth for body and heart and soul,
On Christmas Day in the morning.

If ye would hear the angels sing,
    Christians, think on Him who died,
    Think of your Lord, the crucified,
On Christmas Day in the morning.

Spice it warm, and spice it strong,
    Christians, rise! the world is gray,
    And rough is the road, and short is the day,
Yet Christmas comes in the morning.
                    DORA GREENWELL.

CHRISTMAS-TIME.

THE happy Christmas-time draws near;
    Full are the hours of glad expectancy;
Dull cares and common for a while have flown,
And through the household-music creeps a tone
    Of hushed and hidden glee;
For still the blessed joy-time of the year
Is sacred unto thoughts of all the heart holds dear.

    The children run about,
        Trying vainly to keep out
    The mischievous shining from their eyes
        That might reveal the tale—
    Full of some wonderful surprise,
    Which none must venture even to surmise
        Till Christmas lifts the veil.
The spirit of loving industry,
Of happy secrets, and of merry mystery,
Fills all the house, till every guarded room
With hidden flowers of love begins to bloom.

    Even the little ones are busy too,
    There is so much to do!
    They fetch and carry, flutter here and there.

With most important air,
And choose their longest stockings out,
With never a thought of doubt,
The good Kriss Kringle's bounty to receive.
All things they hope, all things believe;
May God keep whole
The sweet child-trust in each young, innocent soul!

    The dear house-mother smiles,
      And does not seem to see,
    Herself entangled in the wiles
      Of Christmas mystery.
With well-feigned sober mien,
And lip and brow serene,
Her cunningest devices she applies
To slip the scrutiny of eager eyes,
And hides away upon the closet-shelf
Parcels of shape and size
That could have only come from Santa Claus himself.

  The busy hum pervades
    Kitchen as well as hall,
  And dainties hidden from the schoolboy's raids
    Come forth in answer to the Christmas call.
    Odors of spice and plum
    From the well-filled pantry come;
    And sounds suggestive (as the eggs they beat,
    Now chop the apples) tempt the little feet,
    Brighten the laughing eyes,
    And set small mouths a-watering
    For Christmas cake and pies.

The blessed day draws nigh;
The ruddy lads come in, their arms piled high
With Christmas boughs of cedar, fir, and pine,
Red-berried holly and green ivy-vine.
The incense-like perfume
Hallows each happy room.
The house is beautiful with Christmas cheer;
It is the gay time of the year!

O Christ! who on this Christmas morn,
  Long years ago,
      While angels sang the chime
      For the first Christmas-time,
Of a poor maid wast born,
      And laid'st Thy kingly head
      Beneath the humble shed,
  Where sad-eyed oxen feed on bruisèd corn,
And milch-kine for their weanlings low,—
  O Christ! be pitiful this day!
Let none un-Christmassed go;
    Let no poor wretch in vain for help implore,
    Let none from any door,
    Unwarmed, unfed,
    No kind word said,
    Helpless, be turned away.
    For Thine own sake, we pray!

                KATE NEELY FESTELLIS.

THE CHILD ANGEL.

A LITTLE old fellow was peering about--
He dressed rather shabby, but looked well and stout,
Except that his countenance wore a tired look,
So busy he'd been in his far-away nook;
In work to his elbows day in and day out—
No danger of him being laid up with gout—
But what kind of labor no one had he told,
He looked as if rags and old iron he sold,
Yet no one had ever once seen him stoop down
And pick up such old things as those from the ground;
Although he'd been hanging about now for days,
And looking and acting in many queer ways;
To-day he was listening in people's back-yards
And seemed to be writing some names down on cards;
He peeped in at windows when no one was near,
And sometimes he put to the keyholes his ear;
He looked rather simple, but quiet and good,
And never asked questions nor begged any food;
So careful he was not to cough or to sneeze,
He'd stoop behind fences or dodge behind trees
If any one watched him from window or door,
And hastily left for new fields to explore.
But now it was nearing the close of the day,
And children were out for an exercise play;

The days in the winter are short, at their best,
But a romp they must have ere retiring to rest.
Away in the east is a dim little star,
That warns them dark night is advancing afar;
And so with a will they all frolicked and ran,
Till some one discovered the little old man;
They one and all hailed him with riotous shout,
The boys and girls hastily gathering about;
He tried to escape them, ran into a court,
But on they went after him, bent on some sport;
One naughty boy at him some snow roughly threw—
The little man muttered, "Ah! if you but knew!"
"Shame! shame!" the rest cried out, "Don't do that
    again;
We can have lots of fun without giving him pain!"
So now all surround him and gently they teased;
One playfully from him his knotty cane seized,
One stuck an old quill in his hat's broken brim;
He made no resistance, but looked rather grim;
They tried to unbind an immense heavy pack
That securely was strapped on his old, crooked back
They strove to unbutton a large, brownish coat
That covered his form from his heels to his throat;
They pin strips of paper all over his back,
And a placard, "For Sale," upon him they tack;
And he remained patient and quiet through all,
Till some one again hit him with a snow-ball.
Now, this was as naughty as naughty could be,
And greatly it pained him such conduct to see;
'Twas wonderful how the old man kept so still,
He ought to have boxed that boy's ears with a will;

And all the good children were thinking the same.
For they with one impulse in anger exclaim,
" For shame! you bad boy, to so roughly entreat
A destitute stranger alone in the street;
Maybe he has neither a friend nor a home;
If you know what's best, you'll just let him alone!"
Then, seeing how pleased grew his sad countenance
They drew somewhat nearer; to his side they advance
And stroked his fat fingers, took off all the things
The boys had pinned on him, still calling them
  " wings ";
And here, once again, he repeated quite low,
" I wonder what each one will say when they know!"
And now they were silent, no one spoke a word;
So, thinking perhaps that now he could be heard,
Said he: " 'Tis the privilege of every old man
To tell a good story whenever he can,
And if you'll be quiet a moment or two,
I'll tell you one that I believe is quite true."
Now all were attentive, with eyes and with ears,
Forgetting their play and neglecting their jeers;
His voice was as sweet as the tones of a bell,
When for the first time on their ears it fell,
As he opened his lips this tale to impart,
The moral of which he hoped, would touch every
  heart.

"A poor little girl on a door-step sat,
Carefully feeding some bread to her cat;
A nice slice of sponge-cake lay on her knee.

Some one had given her for her own tea;
When little kitty for more bread would mew,
Sweetly she'd tell her, 'I'm hungry, too;
This piece of sweet cake, you know is my treat,
For little have I of such food to eat!'
When kitty's last morsel was swallowed from sight,
Grace opened her mouth to take a big bite
Of her own supper, when, raising her eyes,
She saw standing near a child her own size,
But oh! so much poorer! his clothes were all torn,
His feet almost barefoot, his shoes were so worn;
He spoke in a whisper, so low and so sweet,
'I am very hungry, please give me to eat.'
She offered him quickly all that she had,
And then very sweetly to him she said:
'Not only my supper, but take kitty, too,
So you'll have some one nice to love you.'
The kind words had scarcely escaped from her lips,
When, the boy disappearing, in the same place there sits
An angel—so lovely, so radiantly white—
Who kissed her white forehead and vanished from sight.
And so, little children, hereafter beware
How you're treating a stranger; you may unaware
Abuse God's dear angels, or—maybe—now think—
Some one else of importance!" he said, with a wink.
One sweet little maiden, quite timid and mild,
Asked: "Are you an angel?" "Well, no, my dear child,
For you see I've no wings as they have to fly,

And yet, let me tell you, I live in the sky!"
"Oh! please, sir, do tell us now what is your name
These rude boys, I fear, are sadly to blame."
He straightened himself to remarkable size,
Which made them all open their eyes in surprise;
His face, that before had looked furrowed and old,
Now seemed very ruddy and fresh-like and bold;
He threw back his mantle, disclosing to view
A beautiful overcoat glistening like dew;
Then laying his finger one side of his nose,
He tried to look solemn—and did, I suppose—
Then waited, what seemed to them all a long pause,
Before he said, softly, "My name's Santa Claus!"
If you could have heard then the wailing and woe,
The girls' "There! we told you!" and the boys'
"Oh! oh! oh!"
I think you'd have felt just as sorry as he,
When down at his feet they knelt penitently,
And promised him, over and over again,
They'd never make sport any more of old men.
"Well, then, I'll forgive you this time! wipe your eyes,
And to-night be prepared for a greater surprise."

Hannah More Kohaus.

THE OLD-TIME BELLS.

OH! bells of joy, how sweet they ring,
    Chiming bells, Christmas bells,
Good news for all once more they bring,
    Happy Christmas bells;

Floating in the morning beam,
Gliding o'er the silent stream,
Turning sadness into gladness
With their tuneful chime.

Hark! the old-time bells,
We love the greeting of the old-time bells,
A Saviour's birth repeating, hear the old-time bells
Oh! joyful tidings, joyful tidings,
Rolling on, rolling on,
Happy Christmas bells.

Oh! bells of peace from God above,
Silver bells, Christmas bells,
Ev'ry tone is full of love,
Happy Christmas bells;
Stealing o'er the vales along,
Waking all the world to song,
Sweetly ringing, pleasure bringing,
In their tuneful chime.

Hark! the old-time bells,
We love the happy greeting of the old-time bells,
A Saviour's birth repeating, hear the old-time bells.
Oh! joyful tidings, joyful tidings,
Rolling on, rolling on,
Happy Christmas bells.

Oh! bells of hope to souls oppressed,
Merry bells, Christmas bells,
Hear them tell of tranquil rest,
Happy Christmas bells.

Cheerily they still resound,
Cheerily we catch the sound,
Glory in the highest, glory!
Oh! the tuneful chime.

Hark! the old-time bells,
We love the happy greeting of the old-time bells,
A Saviour's birth repeating, hear the old-time bells
Oh! joyful tidings, joyful tidings,
Rolling on, rolling on,
Happy Christmas bells.

KITTY'S CHRISTMAS OFFERING.

IT was the prettiest, daintiest little bit of muslin, lace, and embroidery ever put together, with Kitty's own name in one corner, all covered about with tiny leaves, flowers, and tendrils which seemed as if they must have been worked by fairy fingers, and it came tied down by pink ribbons in " Oh! such a lovely box, with four little boys, without much clothes on them, 'cept wings, carrying Christmas greens."

For was not this Christmas morning, and had not Kitty, when asked by grandmamma a month since what she most wanted for a Christmas present, answered, "A 'broidered handkerstuff?"

Yes, grandmamma was the good fairy whose skillful fingers had worked the dainty trifle, and it would be hard to tell what pains those loving fingers would not take to please the little maiden whose winsome looks and words found their way to all hearts.

A proud and happy child was Kitty when she received that wonderful Christmas gift, and when she was dressed for church and nurse had arranged the little handkerchief in her mite of a pocket so the lace edge and embroidered name might show, she felt rather finer and more elegantly dressed than she had ever felt in her little life before.

This was not the first time that Kitty had been to church. For three or four Sundays now she had gone with her father and mother, and so far she had been as quiet and well-behaved as any little five-year-old girl could be. But whether it was the new handkerchief or all the other unusual excitements of the day, Kitty was far more restless that Christmas morning than she had ever been before, and by and by she scrambled to her feet upon the seat, turning so as to face the congregation. Seeing this kept the little woman quiet for a time, her mamma let her stand there during reading of the Scriptures, and Kitty amused herself with gazing about her.

Suddenly she spied several pews off, a gentleman who often came to her papa's house, and whom she liked very much.

"Mr. James never saw my new-put-handkerstuff," said Kitty to herself, when she had smiled at him and nodded her head like any Chinese mandarin. "He might be offended of me if I did not show it to him."

And pulling the little handkerchief from her

pocket she shook it out, and holding it up by two corners as high as her hands could reach, and quite forgetting that she was in church, she called aloud:

"Mr. James, you couldn't afford dis."

Her mamma pulled her down pretty quickly, as you may be sure, but all the young people around began to titter, and even the older and graver people could not help smiling.

When Kitty remembered that she had so forgotten herself, and spoken aloud in church, she was very much mortified, and she laid her head against her mamma's arm, and would not look up again for some time, while two or three big tears of shame stole down to her cheeks.

When she had dried her eyes and could raise her head once more, the minister was talking. Kitty always thought it very strange that such a tall, grave gentleman as the clergyman should talk so much and so loud in church when she was not to be allowed to speak at all.

But now, as she sat gazing up at him and listening, she presently became interested in what he was saying. She could understand a good deal of what he said, and she found that he was telling of a home which some kind ladies had started for poor little sick and crippled children who needed kind care and a comfortable place when they were ill.

People were talking about "hard times" he said, and the ladies who were in charge of the hospital did, indeed, feel that these were "hard times," for they did not receive one-half the money they needed for the wants of sick children. And then he asked that those who were better off and who had many good things to be thankful for that Christmas Day, would give of their abundance for those who were in want.

He spoke, too, a few words to the children of the congregation.

"There is hardly a child here," he said, "who has not some trifle which he or she may spare for these poor little ones who have not such happy, pleasant homes as you have, who have not had such Christmas gifts as most of you have received. Would not each one like to send something which may give pleasure or comfort, which will gladden the heart of some little child like yourselves? And, dear children, remember that any offering you may make this morning is in the name and for the sake of the Baby who was born to-day in Bethlehem—the Saviour Christ who came to give us the best of all Christmas gifts—salvation and everlasting life."

Even the very smallest children present could help, he said, and if it was but done for the love of the dear Jesus who had blessed and called them, it would show they wished to please Him.

Kitty heard, and she was very sure that she did wish to please the dear Jesus whose birthday all loved to keep on this Christmas morning, and as she listened she wished that she, too, could give something for those poor little children who had had no presents.

But what should it be?

She had no toys or picture-books with her there in church, and her pennies were all safe at home in her money-box. If she but had some there, or one or two of the new toys or books, she would give them gladly for the little cripples. There were the gentlemen beginning to pass round the plates for the offerings, and Kitty had not one single thing to give.

As she thought this her eye fell upon the new pocket-handkerchief which lay upon her lap.

Why, she could give this, and how pleased the little children would be. She did not believe that they had ever seen one so pretty, she was sure she never had. But could she give it up, even for these children who had so few pretty things when she had so many?

There was a moment's struggle as the gentleman came slowly up the aisle with the plate, taking from each person present what they could or would give, and the organ played and a sweet voice sang the words, "Inasmuch as ye have done it unto the least of these ye have done it unto me." Then Kitty's mamma saw her carefully fold the little handkerchief, give it one kiss—a good-bye kiss it was, as mamma knew a moment later when the gentleman passed the plate into the pew, and Kitty laid the dainty trifle upon it, and raising eyes swimming in tears, forgot herself once more, and said aloud, "It will do for those little cripples, and I want to help dem."

The gentleman hesitated one moment and glanced at Kitty's papa as the latter laid his contribution upon the plate, but papa, who saw what it all meant, motioned him on.

There was a very suspicious glistening in the eyes
of that old gentleman as he went on, up one side of
the aisle and down the other, bearing the plate with
that tiny morsel of lace and embroidery lying upon
it—the baby's offering—which worked its mission on
its way, telling its own story and opening many a
heart to give more largely and freely than it would
have done but for that silent monitor and example.

Carefully treasured among mamma's dearest pos-
sessions lies the little handkerchief all unknown to
Kitty; but the sum which redeemed it has gone to
buy many a comfort and pleasure for the cripples to
whom Kitty sent her offering.

CHRISTMAS TIDE.

WHEN the merry spring time weaves
    Its peeping bloom and dewy leaves;
When the primrose opes its eye,
And the young moth flutters by;
When the plaintive turtle-dove
Pours its notes of peace and love;
And the clear sun flings its glory bright and wide—
    Yet, my soul will own
    More joy in winter's frown,
And wake with warmer flush at Christmas tide.

    The summer beams may shine
    On the rich and curling vine,
    And the noon-tide rays light up
    The tulip's dazzling cup:

But the pearly mistletoe
And the holly-berries' glow
Are not even by the boasted rose outvied;
For the happy hearts beneath
The green and coral wreath
Love the garlands that are twined at Christmas tide

Let the autumn days produce
Yellow corn and purple juice,
And Nature's feast be spread
In the fruitage ripe and red;
'Tis grateful to behold
Gushing grapes and fields of gold,
When cheeks are browned and red lips deeper dyed
But give, oh! give to me
The winter night of glee,
The mirth and plenty seen at Christmas tide.

The northern gust may howl,
The rolling storm-cloud scowl,
King Frost may make a slave
Of the river's rapid wave,
The snow-drift choke the path,
Or the hail-shower spend its wrath;
But the sternest blast right bravely is defied,
While limbs and spirits bound
To the merry minstrel sound,
And social wood-fire's blaze at Christmas tide.

The song, the laugh, the shout,
Shall mock the storm without;

    And sparkling wine-foam rise
    'Neath still more sparkling eyes;
    The forms that rarely meet
    Then hand to hand shall greet,
And soul pledge soul that leagues too long divide.
    Mirth, friendship, love, and light
    Shall crown the winter's night,
And every glad voice welcome Christmas tide.

    But while joy's echo falls
    In gay and plenteous halls,
    Let the poor and lowly share
    The warmth, the sports, the fare;
    For the one of humble lot
    Must not shiver in his cot,
But claim a bounteous meed from wealth and pride
    Shed kindly blessings round,
    Till no aching heart be found;
And then all hail to merry Christmas tide!

                    ELIZA COOK.

ECHOES FROM BETHLEHEM.

              It was night;
The pulse of human life that through the day
Had bounded on its restless, feverish way,
Was at its lowest ebb, and over all
Omnipotence had tenderly let fall
The robe of slumber. Silence reigned supreme.
The moon's pale flood, with weird and shifting gleam,
Enwrapped the world, while myriad stars above

Bedecked the throne of Him whose name is Love,
And as I gazed from earth to jeweled sky,
It seemed that heaven to earth was drawing nigh.
A fleecy cloud spread far and wide and bright,
Through which the stars shone with redoubled light.
As closer heaven drew near the sleeping world,
I saw the cloud was but the wings unfurled
And luminous of hosts unnumbered, bright,
That covered all the starry arch of night,
Wheeling in shining squadrons swift and free,
And noiseless as the moonbeams on the sea;
In heavenly majesty they marshalled there,
Above a valley clothed in verdure fair,
Where shepherds watched their slumb'ring flocks by
    night,
Nor saw above the gath'ring legions bright.
And then I saw a star, whose steady glow
Illumed the waving trees that murmured low
In the night breeze, and as it moved, behold,
Laden with myrrh and frankincense and gold,
There followed strange men, from a land afar,
With stately mien and eyes fixed on the star;
Their faces shone with hope and wond'ring awe
As steadfastly they gazed, and then I saw
The glowing star stand still and hover o'er
A lowly portal; through the open door
A radiance streamed and mingled with the light
The star rained down, until the shades of night
Were vanquished by the mingled glory there.
Inside, an awe-struck mother, pale and fair,
Bent o'er a manger wherein lay a child,

Who turned an angel's face to her and smiled,
And as He smiled, behold, there burst a sound
From all the shining legions watching 'round
That thrilled the earth, the air, the peopled sky,
And rose in waves of harmony on high,
Until God's universe took up the strain
And sent the echo back to earth again.

THE CHRISTMAS-TREE.

> " Merry, merry Christmas everywhere,
> Cheerily it ringeth through the air."

ONLY by giving gifts can the true meaning of the great gift of peace and good-will be impressed. The old German legend of the origin of the Christmas-tree is full of the spirit of the season. The story introduces two children sitting by the fire one cold winter's night. A timid knock is heard at the door, and the boy runs to open it, to find a child standing outside in the cold and darkness, with no shoes on his feet, and clad in thin, ragged garments. He is shivering with cold, and asks to come in and warm himself. "Yes," cry both the children, "you shall have our place by the fire. Come in." They draw the little stranger to their warm seat, share their supper with him, and give him their bed, while they sleep on the hard bench. In the night they are awakened by strains of sweet music, and looking out see a band of children in shining garments approaching the house. They are playing on golden harps, and the air is full of melody. Suddenly the Stranger child stands beside them, no longer cold and ragged, but clad in silvery light, and His soft voice says, "I was cold, and you took me in. I was hungry, and you fed me. I was tired, and you gave me your bed I am the Christ-child, wandering through the world to bring peace and happiness to the hearts of all good children. As you have given to me, so may this tree every year give rich fruit to you." So saying, he broke a branch from a fir-tree, planted it in the ground and disappeared. But the branch grew into a great tree and every year bore golden fruit for the kind children.

LUCY WHEELOCK.

CHRISTKINDLEIN.

HOW bird-like o'er the flakes of snow
   Its fairy footsteps flew,
And on its soft and childish brow
   How delicate the hue.

And expectation wings its feet
   And stirs its infant smile,
The merry bells their chimes repeat,
   The child stands still the while.

Then clasps in joy its little hand,
   Then marks the Christian dome,
The stranger-child, in stranger land,
   Feels now as if at home.

It runs along the sparkling ground,
  Its face with gladness beams,
It frolics in the blaze around,
  Which from each window gleams.

The shadows dance upon the wall,
  Reflected from the trees,
And from the branches, green and tall
  The glittering gifts it sees.

It views within the lighted hall
  The charm of social love,
Oh! what a joyous festival!
  'Tis sanctioned from above.

But now the childish heart's unstrung,
  "Where is my taper's light?
And why has no evergreen been hung
  With toys for me to-night?

" In my sweet home there was a band
  Of holy love for me,
A mother's kind and tender hand
  Once decked my Christmas-tree.

" Oh! some one take me 'neath the blaze
  Of those light-tapers, do,
And, children, I can join the plays,
  Oh! let me play with you.

" I care not for the prettiest toy,
  I want the love of home,
Oh! let me in your playful joy
  Forget I have to roam."

The little fragile hand is raised,
   It knocks at every gate,
In every window earnest gazed,
   Then 'mid the snow he sat.

"Christkinkle! thou, the children's friend,
   I've none to love me now,
Hast thou forgot my tree to send,
   With lights on every bough?"

The kindlein's hands are numbed with frost,
   Yet press the little cloak,
Then on its breast in meekness crossed
   A sigh the silence broke.

And closer still the cloak it drew
   Around its silken hair,
Its pretty eyes so clear and blue
   Alone defied the air.

Then came another pilgrim child,
   A shining light He held,
The accents fell so sweet and mild,
   All music they excelled.

"I am thy Christmas friend, indeed,
   And once a child like thee,
When all forgot, thou need'st not plead,
   I will adorn thy tree.

"My joys are felt in street or bower,
   My aid is everywhere,
Thy Christmas-tree, my precious flower,
   Here in the open air,

" Shall far outshine those other trees,
   Which caught thine infant eye,"
The stranger-child looks up and sees
   Far in the deep blue sky

A glorious tree, and stars among
   The branches hang their light,
The child, with soul all music, sung,
   " My tree, indeed, is bright."

As 'neath the power of a dream
   The infant closed its eyes,
And troops of radiant angels seem
   Descending from the skies.

The baby to its Christ they bear,
   With Jesus safe to live,
To find a home and treasure there
   Sweeter than earth can give.

                    FRIEDRICH RUCKERT

CHRISTMAS DAY.

A GOOD old-fashioned Chris'mas, with the logs
   upon the hearth,
The table filled with feasters, an' the room a-roar 'ith mirth,
With the stockins' crammed to bu'stin', an' the medders piled 'ith snow—
A good old-fashioned Chris'mas like we had so long ago.

Now, that's the thing I'd like to see ag'in afore 1 did
But Chris'mas in the city here—it's different, oh! my!
With the crowded hustle-bustle of the slushy, noisy street,
An' the scowl upon the faces of the strangers that you meet.

Oh! there's buyin', plenty of it, of a lot o' gorgeous toys:
An' it takes a mint o' money to please modern girls an' boys.
Why, I mind the time a jack-knife an' a toffy lump for me
Made my little heart an' stockin' jus' chock-full o' Chris'mas glee.

An' there's feastin'. Think o' feedin' with these stuck-up city folk!
Why, ye have to speak in whispers, an' ye darsn't crack a joke.
Then remember how the tables looked, all crowded with your kin,
When you couldn't hear a whistle blow across the merry din!

You see, I'm so old-fashioned, like, I don't care much for style,
An' to eat your Chris'mas banquets here I wouldn't go a mile:
I'd rather have, like Solomon, a good yarb-dinner, set
With real old friends, than turkle soup with all the nobs you'd get.

There's my next-door neighbor Gurley—fancy how
    his brows 'u'd lift
If I'd holler " Merry Chris'mas! Caught, old fellow;
    Chris'mas gift!"
Lordy-Lord, I'd like to try it! Guess he'd nearly have
    a fit.
Hang this city stiffness, anyways; I can't get used
    to it.

Then your heart kept a-swellin' till it nearly bu'st
    your side,
An' by night your jaws were achin', with your smile
    four inches wide,
An' your enemy, the wo'st one, you'd grab his hand
    an' say:
" Mebbe both of us was wrong, John; come, let's
    shake, it's Chris'mas Day!"

Mighty little Chris'mas spirit seems to dwell 'tween
    city walls,
Where each snow-flake brings a soot-flake for a
    brother as it falls;
Mighty little Chris'mas spirit! An' I'm a-pinin', don't
    you know,
For a good old-fashioned Chris'mas, like we had so
    long ago.

                ALICE WILLIAMS BROTHERTON.

THE SHEPHERD-BOY'S CAROL.

So long ago, so long ago, a fair-haired shepherd
  boy
Went through the streets of Bethlehem, his face
  alight with joy;
Unheeding all who passed him by, he gayly strode
  along,
And ever from his fresh, young lips there fell this
  strange, sweet song:
      "Glory to God in the highest,
        And on earth peace,
        Good-will to men."

Lightly his shepherd's staff he swung, lightly his scrip
  he bore,
A gladsome smile, an earnest joy, his sun-browned
  features wore,
And often toward the deep blue sky his eyes, as blue,
  were raised,
And all the time his silver voice rang as he upward
  gazed:
      "Glory to God in the highest,
        And on earth peace,
        Good-will toward men."

What mean you now, you shepherd lad? What is
  the song you sing?
Why shine your eyes? Why smile your lips? What
  is the news you bring?

Sing us the song you used to sing, old David's hymn,
    again,
'The Lord my Shepherd is," for we know not this
    wond'rous strain.

Well may ye say a wondrous strain, for, know ye,
    it belongs
To the angelic melodies—'tis one of Heaven's songs!
My voice is weak, these notes to raise; how can a
    shepherd-boy
Tell how the hosts of Heaven sang this holy song of
    joy?

Last night I watched my father's sheep, and ere it
    yet was day
I fell asleep, and in my arms a little lamb there lay,
And as it nestled to my heart, I dreamed that once
    again
My dear dead mother held me close, and sang a sweet
    refrain:
   " Glory to God in the highest,
    And on earth peace,
    Good-will toward men."

Waking, I reached out eager arms, when suddenly
    there fell
Upon my eyes a glorious light, of which I cannot tell,
And all the shining air was full of music, passing
    sweet,
The same strange chant, which, in my dream, had
    made my pulses beat.

And angel voices told a tale, while angel faces
    shone—
A tale of some dear child God gives to-day to be our
    own;
I cannot tell you all, for I am but a simple boy,
But this I know, that all the day I sing, and sing for
    joy:
       "Glory to God in the highest,
        And on earth peace,
        Good-will toward men."

And sure I am this little Child a blessed babe must
    be;
No lamb so white, no brook so pure, no field so sweet
    as He;
No shepherd's staff such help can give, no fold so
    safe from ill,
And this is why, this winter's morn, I sing with heart
    and will:
       "Glory to God in the highest,
        And on earth peace,
        Good-will toward men."

THE GOBLINS.

IN an old abbey town, a long, long while ago there officiated as sexton and gravedigger in the churchyard one Gabriel Grubb. He was an ill-conditioned, cross-grained, surly fellow, who consorted with nobody but himself and an old wicker-bottle which fitted into his large, deep waistcoat pocket.

A little before twilight one Christmas Eve, Gabriel shouldered his spade, lighted his lantern, and betook himself toward the old churchyard, for he had a grave to finish by next morning, and feeling very low, he thought it might raise his spirits, perhaps, if he went on with his work at once.

He strode along until he turned into the dark lane which led to the churchyard—a nice, gloomy, mournful place into which the towns-people did not care to go except in broad daylight, consequently he was not a little indignant to hear a young urchin roaring out some jolly song about a Merry Christmas. Gabriel waited until the boy came up, then rapped him over the head with his lantern five or six times to teach him to modulate his voice. And as the boy hurried away, with his hand to his head, Gabriel Grubb chuckled to himself and entered the churchyard, locking the gate behind him.

He took off his coat, put down his lantern, and getting into an unfinished grave, worked at it for an hour or so with right good will. But the earth was hardened with the frost, and it was no easy matter to break it up and shovel it out. At any other time this would have made Gabriel very miserable, but he was so pleased at having stopped the small boy's singing that he took little heed of the scanty progress he had made when he had finished work for the night, and looked down into the grave with grim satisfaction, murmuring as he gathered up his things:

"Brave lodgings for one, brave lodgings for one,
A few feet of cold earth when life is done."

"Ho! **ho!**" he laughed as he set himself down on a flat tombstone, which was a favorite resting-place of his, and drew forth his wicker-bottle; "A coffin at Christmas! A Christmas box. Ho! ho! ho!"

"Ho! ho! ho!" repeated a voice close beside him.

"It was the echoes," said he, raising the bottle to his lips again.

"It was not," said a deep voice.

Gabriel started up and stood rooted to the spot with terror, for his eyes rested on a form that made his blood run cold.

Seated on an upright tombstone close to him was a strange, unearthly figure. He was sitting perfectly still, grinning at Gabriel Grubb with such a grin as only a goblin could call up.

"What do you here on Christmas Eve?" said the goblin, sternly.

"I came to dig a grave, sir," stammered Gabriel.

"What man wanders among graves on such a night as this?" cried the goblin.

"Gabriel Grubb! Gabriel Grubb!" screamed a wild chorus of voices that seemed to fill the churchyard.

"What have you got in that bottle?" said the goblin.

"Hollands, sir," replied the sexton, trembling more than ever, for he had bought it of the smugglers, and he thought his questioner might be in the excise department of the goblins.

"Who drinks Hollands alone, and in a churchyard on such a night as this?"

"Gabriel Grubb! Gabriel Grubb!" exclaimed the wild voices again.

"And who, then, is our lawful prize?" exclaimed the goblin, raising his voice.

The invisible chorus replied, "Gabriel Grubb! Gabriel Grubb!"

"Well, Gabriel, what do you say to this?" said the goblin, as he grinned a broader grin than before.

The sexton gasped for breath.

"What do you think of this, Gabriel?"

"It's—it's very curious, sir, very curious, sir, and very pretty," replied the sexton, half-dead with fright. "But I think I'll go back and finish my work, sir, if you please."

"Work," said the goblin, "what work?"

"The grave, sir."

"Oh! the grave, eh? Who makes graves at a time when other men are merry, and takes a pleasure in it?"

Again the voices replied, "Gabriel Grubb! Gabriel Grubb!"

"I'm afraid my friends want you, Gabriel," said the goblin.

"Under favor, sir," replied the horror-stricken sexton; "I don't think they can; they don't know me, sir; I don't think the gentlemen have ever seen me."

"Oh! yes, they have. We know the man who struck the boy in the envious malice of his heart because the boy could be merry and he could not."

Here the goblin gave a loud, shrill laugh which the echoes returned twenty-fold.

"I—I am afraid I must leave you, sir," said the sexton, making an effort to move.

"Leave us!" said the goblin; "ho! ho! ho!"

As the goblin laughed he suddenly darted toward Gabriel, laid his hand upon his collar, and sank with him through the earth. And when he had had time to fetch his breath he found himself in what appeared to be a large cavern, surrounded on all sides by goblins ugly and grim.

"And now," said the king of the goblins, seated in the centre of the room on an elevated seat—his friend of the churchyard—"show the man of misery and gloom a few of the pictures from our great storehouses."

As the goblin said this a cloud rolled gradually away and disclosed a small and scantily-furnished but neat apartment. Little children were gathered round a bright fire, clinging to their mother's gown, or gamboling round her chair. A frugal meal was spread upon the table and an elbow chair was placed near the fire. Soon the father entered and the children ran to meet him. As he sat down to his meal the mother sat by his side and all seemed happiness and comfort.

"What do you think of that?" said the goblin.

Gabriel murmured something about its being very pretty.

"Show him some more," said the goblin.

Many a time the cloud went and came, and many a lesson it taught to Gabriel Grubb. He saw that men who worked hard and earned their scanty bread were cheerful and happy. And he came to the conclusion it was a very respectable sort of a world after all. No sooner had he formed it than the cloud closed over the last picture seemed to settle on his senses and lull him to repose. One by one the goblins faded from his sight, and as the last one disappeared he sank to sleep.

The day had broken when he awoke, and found himself lying on the flat gravestone, with the wicker bottle empty by his side. He got on his feet as well as he could, and brushing the frost off his coat, turned his face toward the town.

But he was an altered man, he had learned lessons of gentleness and good-nature by his strange adventures in the goblin's cavern.

CHARLES DICKENS.

A CHRISTMAS CAROL.

THE shepherds went their hasty way
  And found the lowly stable-shed
Where the Virgin-Mother lay,
  And now they checked their eager tread,
For to the Babe, that to her nestling clung,
A mother's song the Virgin-Mother sung.

They told her how a glorious light,
  Streaming from a heavenly throng,
Around them shone, suspending night,
  While sweeter than a mother's song
Blest angels heralded the Saviour's birth,
"Glory to God on high, and peace on earth."

She listened to the tale divine,
   And closer still the Babe she prest,
And while she cried, " the Babe is mine,"
   Joy leapt quick within her breast.
Aye, rose within her like a summer's morn,
Peace, peace on earth, the Prince of Peace is born.

Thou, Mother of the Prince of Peace,
   Poor, simple, and of low estate,
That strife should vanish, battle cease,
   Oh! why should this thy soul elate?
Sweet music's loudest note, the poet's story,
Didst thou ne'er love to hear of fame and glory?

And is not War a youthful king,
   A stately hero clad in mail?
Beneath his footsteps laurels spring,
   Him earth's majestic monarchs hail.
Their friend, their playmate, and his bold, bright eye
Compels the maiden's love-confessing sigh.

" Tell this in some more courtly scene,
   To maids and youths in robes of state
I am a woman poor and mean,
   And therefore is my soul elate.
War is a ruffian, all with guilt defiled
That from the aged father tears his child.

"A murderous fiend, by fiends adored,
   He kills the sire and starves the son,
The husband kills, and from her board
   Steals all his widow's toil had won.
Plunders God's world of beauty, rends away
All safety from the night, all comfort from the day.

" Then wisely is my soul elate,
  That strife should vanish, battle cease,
I'm poor and of low estate,
  The Mother of the Prince of Peace.
Joy rises in me, like a summer's morn,
Peace, peace on earth, the Prince of peace is born."
                                    S. T. COLERIDGE.

SANTA CLAUS' AGENT.

THE day before Christmas dawned frosty and bright,
The bare trees presented a beautiful sight;
From brown, leafless branches the icicles hung
In crystals, resembling a white, silver tongue;
The roofs of the houses all glistened like dew
That lays on the flowers with sun shining through;
The boys and the girls, all wrapped to their eyes,
Stood about on the street, looking up to the skies,
And listening intently, with hand to their ear,
If Santa Claus' reindeers were not somewhere near.
" I see them ! I see them !" one little boy cried,
As a tiny white cloud in the azure he spied;
And he clapped his red hands in sweet childish glee,
And called to the others, " Come on, follow me !"
All eagerly started off on a brisk run—
And to see their legs fly, I tell you, was fun;
Before they arrived at the destined place
(A block down the main street), it proved quite a race:

Every one to be first had striven his best,
And each little face was as red as his vest;
And while they were panting aloud with their might,
They looked up and—behold, no cloud was in sight!
The happy smile faded quite out of each face,
And one of vexation came into its place;
When, all unexpected, a bright little girl—
The only sweet darling whose lip did not curl—
Cried. "Look! look! there they are, just crossing the wire
On the telegraph pole behind the church spire!"
Again they all started pell-mell on a run,
Some slipped on the pavement, and down they did come;
But quick to their rescue the others ran back,
And once more they are off on the reindeers' track.
They went quite a distance down through a long lane,
They must get very near to the pole to see plain;
But gone was their rapture, all flown their delight,
It proved to be only an old battered kite.
So, quite disappointed, they walked to and fro,
Their hands in their pockets, their feet crunching snow;
Said one little fellow, "Real still let us be,
Perhaps we can hear them much better than see."
And then such a clatter they heard, sure enough,
That must be the reindeers on somebody's roof;
So they pulled back their ears and opened their eyes,
But to their amazement, disgust, and surprise,
'Twas only the snow-birds upon the barn roofs

They now had mistaken for reindeers' hoofs.
Now very disheartened back home they all ran;
With heads hanging downward, they bumped 'gainst
 a man,
That none of them noticed before standing round,
Because they weren't looking for things on the
 ground.
Such a queer-looking chap, so round and so fat,
With a long white top-coat and high furry hat;
He had the appearance of being stuffed well
With something unusual, but what, none could tell;
From under his hat peered a little red foot;
From out of a pocket the heel of a boot;
The head of a kitten peeped out from his breast,
But 'twould take too much time to tell you the rest.
He spoke to them kindly: "Well, my little dears,
Pray, tell me the meaning of all these sad tears."
One little boy answered, without any fear,
"We've tried to be good, sir, throughout the whole
 year,
And now we've been looking in the blue sky so
 bright,
To see if dear 'Santa' is coming to-night;
We've now looked all over, but nowhere appears
A thing that resembles the form of reindeers!"
"Of course not, my children [his eyes fairly beam]
You know you can only see them in a dream;
I'm old Santa's agent, and to me he said:
'Tell all the good children to get into bed,
Put some sleep in their eyes, some caps o'er their
 ears,

Then they can see plainly, and hear the reindeers.'"
They gazed at him wondering, with fluttering heart
Their mouths stretched wide open, their feet far
  apart;
Then off for their homes, with a shout full of glee,
They hurried and scampered like caged birds set free.
Then did the queer fellow "Ha! ha!" and "he! he!"
And shrug his broad shoulders and slap his fat knee;
And long ere the stars shone they'd all gone to rest.
Their ears nightcapped over, sleep on their eyes
  pressed,
When lo! and behold! what a sight they did see!
That same jolly fellow, still shaking with glee,
His great-coat still open, his hat fallen back,
And on his broad shoulders an extra large sack,
Crammed full of the finest, most desirable things,
Of every description that Christmas time brings.
His reindeers stood champing outside the house door,
While he tumbled everything down on the floor;
His face fairly radiant with honest delight,
He cried "Merry Christmas! Till morning sleep
  tight."
Then over the housetops of rich and of poor
He flew like the north wind, and stopped at each
  door,
The same words repeating to the lowly and high,
For Santa Claus passes no good children by.
So when Christmas morning all awoke to good cheer
They vowed to be better than ever next year.

HANNAH MORE KOHANS.

AT CHRISTMAS-TIME.

AN EPISODE OF THE RUSSO-TURKISH WAR.

IN his wind-shaken tent the soldier sits,
  Beside him flares an oil lamp smokily,
Whose dim light glooms and flickers on the sheet
Of rustling paper that, with eager eyes
And heart intent he reads. Now with a smile
The flaxen-bearded sunburnt face lights up.
A smile, that in the smiling breeds a pain
Within his yearning heart; the gentle hand
That those sweet, loving words hath traced,
Will he ever again in his protecting clasp
Enfold it? Who can tell? He can but kiss,
With wild intensity, the page that hand
Hath touched. Each line, each word read and
    read.
At last there is no more. With swimming eyes
He looks and drinks her name into his soul.
Yet see those lines with pencil widely ruled
Where largely sprawl big letters helplessly.
What do they say, those baby characters,
So feebly large?

" Loved papa, at Christmas-time
  Will you come home again,
    My own dear papa?"

As he reads this, the tent to him grows darker,
His strong hand trembles and the hot tears burn
In his blue eyes and blur the struggling words.

What need to see? The words are stamped upon
His heart, and his whole soul doth feel them there.
The wind on gusty wings sweeps by, and, lo!
With its wild voice his child's sweet treble mingles in
    accents clear:
> "Loved papa, at Christmas-time
>   Will you come home again,
>   My own dear papa?"

And now his head is bowed into his hands,
His brave heart for a moment seems to climb
Into his throat and choke him. Hark! what sound
Thus sharply leaps among and slays the sad
Weird voices of the autumn night with shrill
And sudden blast? The bugle calls, "To arms!"
And startled sleepers, at its fierce appeal,
Half-dreaming, clutch their swords, and gasping
    wake.
How many soon to sleep again in death!
And on the father's heart the pealing cry
Strikes cold as ice, though soldier there's none
    braver,
For still above the bugle's thrilling breath
That pleading child-voice sweetly calls:
> "Loved papa, at Christmas-time
>   Will you come home again,
>   My own dear papa?"

Across a rough hillside the light of dawn
Doth coldly creep with ruthless touch revealing
All that by darkness had been hid, and there

Amongst the stalwart forms that stiffening lie
Upon the blood-soaked ground, where they lie the
 thickest
There is one found with flaxen hair and beard
Dark-dyed with gore, a bullet in the heart!
A crumpled paper in his hand was clutched,
'Gainst the cold lips his right hand did press
Some childish writing, by his life-blood stained.
What are the words? One scarce can read them now
 " Loved papa, at Christmas-time
  Will you come home again,
   My own dear papa?"

A LETTER TO SANTA CLAUS.

"PUT a 'velop on it, and write his name, and put in the pos'-office," insisted Polly.

"Polly, what on earth is it?" asked Mattie, looking at the half-sheet of letter paper, with queer ink-lines and cross tracks all over it.

"It's a letter I've writ to Santa Claus," said Polly, with a very serious air.

Mattie's black eyes danced with fun as she looked from the letter to the earnest face of the writer.

"Billy," she exclaimed, "come here and see what Polly's been doing."

"He may look," said Polly, "but I don't want any body else to know."

Billy was one of those boys who can laugh inside and not let a sound escape. He looked at the letter.

"It's just the thing," he said. "I'll sign her name to it."

"And I'll do it up," said Mattie.

"It's got to go," said Billy, "and if it gets to him he may come," though father and mother, and even Mattie had said Santa Claus is not coming to our house "this year."

This was the reason why 'Squire Leadenway, on the day before Christmas, gave his team a rest right in front of the Lummis house. He had not seen anybody yet, but a small, clear voice seemed to almost come up out of the snow:

"Mister!" it said, "wait, please!"

"Hullo!" said 'Squire Leadenway, heartily, "who are you? What do you want?"

"I'm Polly Lummis. It's a pos'-office."

She held up the white envelope as she spoke, and he could now look down from his load of bags of grain into her round, rosy, and eager little face. His hand, covered by a great thick, yarn mitten, went right out and took the letter.

"Post-office?" he said. "Yes. No stamp. Sakes alive! Santa Claus? Guess it doesn't need any stamp. I'll take it, Polly."

"Will it get him?" asked Polly.

"Hope it will," he said, emphatically. "I declare! Santa Claus! You thought you'd write to him, eh?"

"'Cause he isn't coming to our house," she said.

"That's bad," said the 'Squire. "He ought to come. Why, I'd like to see him myself."

"Thank you, sir," said Polly. "I hope it'll get him."

She darted back to the gate, and 'Squire Leadenway drove on to the village, chuckling to himself: "Fat little chub. Christmas. Well, now. Children of her size are kind o' sca'ce."

A little later a squad of men were standing by the counter in McGonegal's store. At that moment the door flew open, and 'Squire Leadenway stamped slowly in. He was an important man, and all were ready to say "good morning" to him, but he spoke first to the postmaster:

"McGonegal, there, does that call for a two-cent stamp or a one-cent, or will you take it out in trade?"

"Santa Claus!" exclaimed the astonished postmaster. "He doesn't live anywhere round here. What does it mean?"

It means Polly Lummis—little chub 'bout's high as a grasshopper — stopped me in front of their house. Said Santa Claus wasn't coming if the letter didn't get him. I'd give something to know what's inside," said the 'Squire.

"I have some curiosity myself," remarked Dr. Link.

"I haven't," said Elder Group, with firmness. "It's a childish superstition."

"Open it comes!" exclaimed Judge Hopper, and it was curious to see those gray heads and wrinkled faces crowding toward that piece of paper covered with curious signs and pictures.

"It needs an interpreter," said Dr. Link. "It appears to be written in an unknown tongue."

"I'm not so sure of that," remarked Judge Hopper. "Guess I'm Santa Claus enough to take it home, anyway, and show it to my wife."

Everybody in the store saw it first; and the Judge showed it to three men and four women on his way to his own house.

"Sho!" said Mrs. Hopper when she saw it, "your name isn't Santa Claus, nor mine either. What made you keep it?"

"Because, Ellen, I thought you might see some fun in it."

"Sho! nonsense! You're too old a man to do any practical joking. So is 'Squire Leadenway. Did he write that scrawl, or did you?"

"Polly Lummis gave it to him. 'Tisn't a scrawl, exactly. I've been trying to make out what she means. That's a doll's face, and those must be sticks of candy."

"You don't say. She's a little thing."

Mrs. Hopper sat down with Polly's letter in her lap. It was difficult to read, beyond a doubt, for it made her wipe her spectacles three times before she finished it. She got up quickly and went up-stairs. She walked straight to an old bureau, unlocked a drawer and pulled it out. It was full of children's toys. "Twelve years ago," she said, "and I've never taken 'em out any year till the night before Christmas." Then all that was in the drawer came out upon the floor, and she sat down by the heap she had made.

Polly Lummis, now that her letter was gone, was

quite sure Santa Claus would call at the post-office and ask if there was anything for him. Billy piled up logs in the sitting-room fireplace after supper until the family had to push back their chairs and sit by the table. There they sat and talked and laughed about the apples and nuts they meant to have when next Christmas Eve should come, and about all the good stories they had ever heard that belonged to Santa Claus and to Christmas, until the forestick broke down in a great shower of sparks, and Mrs. Lummis said it was bed-time.

When Polly had been some two hours asleep, or apparently so, something very queer came. It was not a dream, for it broke right in through a great beautiful dream she was having about Santa Claus reading a letter, and it woke her up. She was sure she heard something. It was a slow crunch, crunch, crunch on the path from the road to the house. She lay as still as a mouse, whispering to herself, " He got it, he got it, I know he got it. That's Santa Claus out there." It was not he, but it was Judge Hopper, all wrapped up, trying to walk stealthily.

" Ellen," said he to a lady back in the snow-drift, " I hung the satchel on the door-knob. They're all a-bed and asleep."

Polly, wide awake, listening, heard another crunch, crunch, crunch, this time very heavy.

" He's come again," she said to herself. " He forgot something, and he had to go back after it."

Once more it was not Santa Claus, only 'Squire Leadenway, with a turkey in one hand and a ham in the other. He put them on the door-step, and got back into the road again, saying to himself:

"I wouldn't have anybody know it, and be called Santa Claus the rest of my life, but Polly'll have a good dinner for herself and her folks."

He barely reached his sleigh, hitched a little distance up the road, in time to escape being seen by a man who came from the direction of the village.

"There he is," said Polly, "crunch, crunch, again."

"It's all I can afford," said Elder Group; "but a quarter-eagle can buy something. I'm glad somebody else has been here," he murmured, as he took out of his pocket a little faded blue silk bag and hung it on the door-knob.

He had hardly passed McGonegal's door when the postmaster came into the street, dragging a well-loaded new sled.

"I was caught in my own trap. I said I'd give Polly the sled if they'd load it. And here I am playing Santa Claus when I ought to be in bed. But then I'm postmaster, and Polly's letter was delivered. I'd like to see Polly, though, when she opens the door in the morning."

Mr. and Mrs. Lummis were up first and arranged a few Christmas surprises, although they had said Santa Claus was not coming. It seemed as if all had found, as they looked at their gifts, as much Christmas as they wished. when suddenly Polly shouted:

"Santa Claus was here last night. I heard him."

"Where was he?" asked Billy.

"Out front of the house."

"Let's go and see if his reindeer left any hoof-marks," said Mattie.

"The letter got him! The letter got him!" shouted Polly.

There was a great deal of Christmas when the gifts were all brought into the sitting-room. And the next time Polly went into the village it seemed as if everybody knew her and had a laugh ready.

WILLIAM O. STODDARD.

CHRISTMAS BELLS.

HARK! the bells of Christmas ringing,
All abroad their echoes flinging,
Wider still and wider winging
  On the waste of wintry air!
On their solemn, swift vibrations,
Rapture, rapture through the nations,
Rapture, tell their glad pulsations
  Million blissful bosoms share.

Every bell to every hammer
Answers with a joyous clamor,
Answers, till from out the glamor
  Of the ages far and dim,
Till from Bethlehem's stable lowly,
Fair as moonrise, opening slowly,
Streams of radiance, pure and holy,
  Down the brightening centuries swim.

Then the bells ring fine and tender,
And from out that far-off splendor,
Veiled in light no dreams could lend her,
   Lo! the virgin-mother mild,
Pale from guiltless pain unspoken,
Calm in faith's deep trust unbroken,
Bright with Heaven's unconscious token,
   Bends above her wondrous child.

Still the bells ring softly, sweetly,
Mingling all their chimes so meetly,
Tracing all my soul completely,
   Till the rosy clouds divide!
And o'er Bethlehem's mountains hoary
Bursts a strange celestial glory,
Swells a sweet seraphic story,
   Trembling o'er the pastures wide.

Glory! Glory! God descending,
Weds with man in bliss unending,
Hark! the ecstatic choirs attending
   Smite their lyres with tempest sound,
Shout! Old Discord's reign is riven,
Peace on earth! good-will is given!
Shout the joy through highest Heaven!
   Make the crystal spheres resound!

Earth's sad wails of woe and wrangling,
Like wild bells in night-storms jangling,
Now their jarring tones untangling
   In some deep harmonious rhyme,

Touched by Love's own hand supernal,
Hush their dissonance infernal,
Catch the rhythmic march eternal,
    Throbbing through the pulse of time.

Lo! the Babe, where glad they found Him
By the chrismal light that crowned Him !
See the shaggy shepherds round Him,
    Round His manger kneeling low !
See the star-led magi speeding,
Priest and scribe the record reading,
Craft and hate each omen heeding,
    Brooding swift the direful blow !

Vain the wrath of kings conspiring !
Vain the malice demons firing !
On the nations long desiring,
    Lo ! at last the Day-Star shines !
Earth shall bless the hour that bore Him
Unborn empires fall before Him,
Unknown climes and tribes adore Him,
    In ten thousand tongues and climes.

Hark! the Christmas bells resounding,
Earth's old jargon all confounding !
Round the world their tumult bounding
    Spreads Immanuel's matchless fame !
Million hands their offerings bringing,
Million hearts around Him clinging,
Million tongues hosanna singing,
    Swell the honors of His name !

Crown Him, monarchs, seers, and sages!
Crown Him, bards in deathless pages!
Crown Him King of all the ages!
   Let the mighty anthem rise.
Hark! the crash of tuneful noises!
Hark! the children's thrilling voices!
Hark! the world in song rejoices
   Till the chorus shakes the skies!

Living Christ, o'er sin victorious,
Dying Lamb all meritorious,
Rising God, forever glorious,
   Take our songs and hearts, we pray.
May we Thee by faith descrying,
On Thy death for life relying,
Rise to rapture never dying,
   Rise with Thee in endless day.

GEORGE LANSING TAYLOR.

NEW YEAR

SONG FOR THE NEW YEAR

OLD Time has turned another page
   Of eternity and truth ;
He reads with a warning voice to age,
   And whispers a lesson to youth.

A year has fled o'er heart and head
   Since last the Yule log burned ;
And we have a task to closely ask,
   What the bosom and brain have learned ?

Oh ! let us hope that our sands have run
   With wisdom's precious grains ;
Oh ! may we find that our hands have done
   Some work of glorious pains.

Then a welcome and cheer to the merry New Year
   While the holly gleams above us ;
With a pardon for the foes who hate,
   And a prayer for those who love us.

We may have seen some loved ones pass
   To the land of hallowed rest ;
We may miss the glow of an honest brow
   And the warmth of a friendly breast.

But if we nursed them while on earth,
  With hearts all true and kind,
Will their spirits blame the sinless mirth
  Of those true hearts left behind?

No, no! it were not well or wise
  To mourn with endless pain;
There's a better world beyond the skies,
  Where the good shall meet again.

Then a welcome and cheer to the merry New Year
  While the holly gleams above us;
With a pardon for the foes who hate,
  And a prayer for those who love us.

Have our days rolled on serenely free
  From sorrow's dim alloy?
Do we still possess the gifts that bless
  And fill our souls with joy?

Are the creatures dear still clinging near?
  Do we hear loved voices come?
Do we gaze on eyes whose glances shed
  A halo round our home?

Oh! if we do, let thanks be poured
  To Him who hath spared and given,
And forget not o'er the festive board
  The mercies held from Heaven.

Then a welcome and cheer to the merry New Year
  While the holly gleams above us!
With a pardon for the foes who hate,
  And a prayer for those who love us.

       ELIZA COOK.

THE NEW YEAR.

HARK! the cock crows, and yon bright star
Proclaims the day himself's not far.
With him old Janus doth appear,
Peeping into the future year,
With such a look as seems to say,
The prospect is not good that way.
Thus do we rise ill sights to see,
And 'gainst ourselves to prophesy,
When the prophetic fear of things
A more tormenting mischief brings,
More full of soul-tormenting gall
Than direst mischiefs can befall.
But stay! but stay! methinks my sight
Better informed by clearer light,
Discerns sereneness in that brow
That all contracted seemed but now.
His reversed face may show distaste
And frown upon the ills are past.
But that which this way looks is clear
And smiles upon the new-born year
He looks, too, from a place so high,
The year lies open to his eye,
And all the moments open are
To the exact discoverer.
Yet more and more he smiles upon
The happy revolution.
Why should we then suspect or fear
The influences of a year,

So smiles upon us the first morn
And speaks us good so soon as born?
Plague out! the last was ill enough,
This cannot but make better proof.
Or, at the worst, as we brushed through
The last, why so we may this, too.
And then the next in reason should
Be super-excellently good.
For the worst ills (we daily see)
Have no more perpetuity
Than the best fortunes that do fall,
Which also bring us wherewithal,
Longer their being to support
Than those do of the other sort.
And who has one good year in three
And yet repines at destiny,
Appears ungrateful in the case
And merits not the good he has.
Then let us welcome the New Guest
With lusty brimmers of the best.
Mirth always should Good Fortune meet
And render e'en disaster sweet,
And though the Princess turn her back,
Let us but line ourselves with sack.
We better shall by far hold out,
Till the next year she face about.

COLTON.

THE OLD YEAR.

WAIL, winter Winds, o'er moor and fell,
　　The year is dying. Hark! The bell
Rings out amid the falling snow,
'Good-bye, old friend, for thou must go;
　　　　　　Good-bye, Old Year.'

Good-bye, Old Year, thy life is done.
Since first thy light upon me shone,
The blissful hopes that fill'd my heart
Are wither'd all, and all depart
　　　　　　With thee, Old Year.

With bitter tears my eyes are wet;
My heart is sad with vain regret
For all the good that I had thought
To do, for ill that I have wrought
　　　　　　In thee, Old Year.

Where are the friends that side by side
With me have walk'd, the true and tried?
Gone! like the snow, that, fair and white,
Fell o'er the land thy birthday night—
　　　　　　All gone, Old Year!

Where are the flowers that brightly bloom'd
In thy young life, and earth perfumed?
Gone! with the winter's frosty breath,
And lying, like our friends, in death—
　　　　　　In death, Old Year!

But soft! thy heart beats faint and slow;
Thine eyes are dim, thy pulse is low;
One parting glance; thy life is o'er,
The New Year stands within the door.
    Good-bye, Old Year!
       VIOLET FULLER.

COASTING NEW YEAR'S EVE.

FROM the quaint old farm-house, nestling **warmly**
 'Neath its overhanging thatch of snow,
Out into the moonlight troop the children,
 Filling all the air with music **as they go,**
Gliding, sliding, down the hill,
Never minding cold nor chill,
O'er the silvered moon-lit snow,
Swift as arrow from the bow,
With a rush of mad delight
Through the crisp air of the **night,**
Speeding far out o'er the plain,
Trudging gayly up again
To where the firelight's ruddy **glow**
Turns to gold the silver snow.
Finer sport who can conceive
Than that of coasting New Year's Eve
Half the fun lies in the fire
That seems to brighter blaze and higher
Than any other of the year,
As though his dying hour to cheer,
And at the same time greeting give

To him who has a year to live.
'Tis built of logs of oak and pine,
Filled in with branches broken fine;
It roars and crackles merrily;
The children round it dance with glee:
They sing and shout and welcome in
The New Year with a joyous din
That rings far out o'er hill and dale,
And warns the watchers in the vale
'Tis time the church bells to employ
To spread the universal joy.

Then the hill is left in silence
　　As the coasters homeward go,
And the crimson of the fire-light
　　Fades from off the trodden snow.

So the years glide by as swiftly
　　As the sleds rush down the hill,
And each new one as it cometh
　　Bringeth more of good than ill.

DIRGE FOR THE YEAR.

ORPHAN hours, the year is dead,
　　Come and sigh, come and weep
Merry hours, smile instead,
　　For the year is but asleep;
See, it smiles as it is sleeping,
Mocking your untimely weeping.

As an earthquake rocks a corse
  In its coffin in the clay,
So white Winter, that rough nurse,
  Rocks the dead—cold year to-day;
Solemn hours! wail aloud
For your mother in her shroud.

As the wild air stirs and sways
  The tree-swung cradle of a child,
So the breath of these rude days
  Rocks the year;—be calm and mild,
Trembling hours; she will arise
With new love within her eyes,

January gray is here,
  Like a sexton by her grave;
February bears the bier,
  March with grief doth howl and rave,
And April weeps,—but, O ye hours!
Follow with May's fairest flowers.

Percy Bysshe Shelley

A NEW YEAR'S CHIME.

Toll! toll! toll!
  For the old year slowly dying,
    Grim, gaunt, sere,
On the breast of Time now lying.
  Hopes of youth are fleeting,
  Hearts with care are beating.
Ho! ye wardens of the bells,
    Toll! toll! toll!
Toll for Earth's enticing fashion.

Toll for Strife's unholy passion,
Toll for Friendship unrequited,
Toll for Hope's enchantments blighted,
Toll for Love's fond pledges broken,
Toll for Want and Woe unspoken,
Toll for Mourners sadly weeping,
Toll for Sin's vast harvest reaping:
  Toll! toll! toll!
Toll that, while the world shall stand,
Sin and Woe shall fill the land!
  Toll! toll! toll!

  Ring! ring! ring!
A welcome to the bright New Year!
  Life, Hope, Joy,
On his radiant brow appear!
 Hearts with love are thrilling,
 Homes with bounty filling.
Ho! ye wardens of the bells,
  Ring! ring! ring!
Ring for Winter's bracing hours,
Ring for birth of Spring and Flowers,
Ring for Summer's fruitful treasure,
Ring for Autumn's boundless measure,
Ring for hands of generous giving,
Ring for vows of nobler living,
Ring for truths of tongue or pen,
Ring, " Peace on earth, good-will toward men."
  Ring! ring! ring
Ring, that this glad year may see
Earth's accomplished jubilee!
  Ring! ring! ring!

THE NEW YEAR.

RING, bells, from every lofty height
An infant fair is born to-night;
Ring far and wide, ring full and clear,
To welcome in the glad New Year.

"The king is dead; long live the king!"
They said of old, and so we sing.
The Old Year's gone to his repose,
There let him rest beneath the snows.

Behind us, with the year that's gone,
Lie countless sins that we have done.
With joy we cast all care away
And pass into a newer day.

New day, new life. whose noble deed
Will all our sinful years succeed,
A life of action, great and strong,
To cancel all we've done of wrong.

Ring, joyous bells! our hearts beat high
With faith and hope. Beyond the sky
Perchance the angels stand and wait
To catch the sound at Heaven's gate!

And echoing each silver tone,
Sing songs of praise around the Throne.
Ring, happy bells, to us is given
Still longer to prepare for Heaven.

VIOLET FULLER.

REJOICINGS UPON THE NEW YEAR'S COM-
ING OF AGE.

THE Old Year being dead, and the New Year coming of age, which he does, by calendar law as soon as the breath is out of the old gentleman's body nothing would serve the young spark, but he must give a dinner upon the occasion, to which all the Days in the year were invited. The Festivals, whom he deputed as his stewards, were mightily taken with the notion. They had been engaged time out of mind, they said, in providing mirth and good cheer for mortals below, and it was time they should have a taste of their own bounty.

It was stiffly debated among them whether the Facts should be admitted. Some said the appearance of such lean, starved guests, with their mortified faces, would pervert the ends of the meeting. But the objection was overruled by Christmas Day, who had a design upon Ash Wednesday (as you shall hear), and a mighty desire to see how the old Domine would behave himself in his cups. Only the Vigils were requested to come with their lanterns to light the gentlefolk home at night.

All the Days came. Covers were provided for three hundred and sixty-five guests at the principal table, with an occasional knife and fork at the sideboard for the Twenty-ninth of February.

Cards of invitation had been issued. The carriers were the Hours; twelve little merry, whirligig foot pages that went all round and found out the persons invited, with the exception of Easter Day, Shrove Tuesday, and a few such movables, who had lately shifted their quarters.

Well, they all met at last, foul Days, fine Days, all sorts of Days, and a rare din they made of it. There was nothing but, "Hail, fellow Day! well met!" only Lady Day seemed a little scornful. Yet some said Twelfth Day cut her out, for she came all royal and glittering and Epiphenous. The rest came in green, some in white, but old Lent and his family were not yet out of mourning. Rainy Days came in dripping, and sunshiny days laughing. Wedding Day was there in marriage finery. Pay Day came late, and Doomsday sent word he might be expected.

April Fool took upon himself to marshal the guests, and May Day, with that sweetness peculiar to her, proposed the health of the host. This being done, the lordly New Year from the upper end of the table returned thanks. Ash Wednesday, being now called upon for a song, struck up a carol, which Christmas Day had taught him. Shrovetide, Lord Mayor's Day, and April Fool next joined in a glee, in which all the Days, chiming in, made a merry burden.

All this while Valentine's Day kept courting pretty May, who sat next him, slipping amorous *billet-doux* under the table till the Dog Days began to be jealous and to bark and rage exceedingly.

At last the Days called for their cloaks and great coats, and took their leaves. Shortest Day went off in a deep black fog that wrapped the little gentleman all round. Two Vigils—so watchmen are called in Heaven—saw Christmas Day safe home; they had been used to the business before. Another Vigil—a stout, sturdy patrol, called the Eve of St. Christopher—seeing Ash Wednesday in a condition little better than he should be, e'en whipt him over his shoulders, pick-a-pack fashion, and he went floating home singing:

"On the bat's back do I fly,"

and a number of old snatches besides. Longest Day set off westward in beautiful crimson and gold; the rest, some in one fashion, some in another; but Valentine and pretty May took their departure together in one of the prettiest silvery twilights a Lover's Day could wish to set in.

CHARLES LAMB.

THE OLD AND THE NEW YEAR

OLD YEAR.

SPARE her at least; look, you have taken from me
    The Present, and I murmur not, nor moan;
The Future, too, with all her glorious promise;
    But do not leave me utterly alone.

Spare me the Past; for, see, she cannot harm you,
    She lies so white and cold, wrapped in her shroud;
All, all my own; and, trust me, I will hide her
    Within my soul, nor speak to her aloud.

I folded her soft hands upon her bosom,
  And strewed my flowers upon her, they still live;
Sometimes I like to kiss her closed white eyelids,
  And think of all the joy she used to give.

Cruel indeed it were to take her from me;
  She sleeps, she will not wake—no fear—again;
And so I laid her, such a gentle burthen,
  Quietly on my heart to still its pain.

I do not think that any smiling Present,
  Any vague Future, spite of all her charms,
Could ever rival her. You know you laid her,
  Twelve fleeting moons ago, then living, in my arms.

NEW YEAR.

Do not crouch to-day, and worship
  The old Past, whose life is fled;
Hush your voice to tender reverence,
  Crowned she lies, but cold and dead;
For the Present reigns our monarch,
  With an added weight of hours;
Honor him, for he is mighty!
  Honor him, for he is ours!

See the shadows of her heroes
  Girt around his cloudy throne;
Every day the ranks are strengthened
  By great hearts to her unknown;
Noble things the great Past promised,
  Holy dreams, both strange and new;

But the present shall fulfill them,
  What she promised he shall do.

He inherits all her treasures,
  He is heir to all her fame,
And the light that lightens round him
  Is the lustre of her name;
He is wise with all her wisdom,
  Living, on her grave he stands,
On his brow he bears her laurels,
  And her harvests in his hands.

Coward, if we should his glory dim,
  Can he reign and conquer?
Let us fight for him as nobly
  As our fathers fought for her.
God, who crowns the dying ages,
  Bids him rule, and us obey—
Bids us cast our lives before him,
  Bids us serve the great To-day.
        ADELAIDE ANNE PROCTER.

PET AND HER CAT.

NOW, Pussy, I've something to tell you
  You know it is New Year's Day,
The big folks are down in the parlor,
  And mamma is just gone away.

We are all alone in the nursery,
  And I want to talk to you, dear,

So you must come and sit by me,
  And make believe you hear.

You see there's a new year coming,
  It only begins to-day,
Do you know I was often naughty
  In the year that is gone away?

You know I have some bad habits,
  I'll mention just one or two,
But there really is quite a number
  Of naughty things that I do.

You see, I don't learn my lessons,
  And, oh! I do hate them so,
I doubt if I know any more to-day
  Than I did a year ago.

Perhaps I am awfully stupid,
  They say I'm a dreadful dunce.
How would you like to learn spelling?
  I wish you could try it once.

And don't you remember Christmas—
  'Twas naughty, I must confess—
But while I was eating my dinner
  I got two spots on my dress.

And they caught me stealing the sugar,
  But I only got two little bits,
When they found me there in the closet,
  And frightened me out of my wits.

And, Pussy, when people scold me,
  I'm always so sulky then,
If they only would tell me gently,
  I never would do it again.

O Pussy! I know I am naughty,
  And often it makes me cry,
I think it would count for something,
  If they knew how hard I try.

But I'll try again in the New Year,
  And, oh! I shall be so glad
If I only can be a good little girl
  And never do anything bad!

ST. VALENTINE'S DAY

VALENTINE'S DAY.

HAIL to thy returning festival, old Bishop Valentine! Great is thy name in the rubric, thou venerable Arch-flamen of Hymen. Immortal Go-between; who and what manner of person art thou? Art thou but a name, typifying the restless principle which impels poor humanity to seek perfection in union? Mysterious personage! like unto thee, assuredly, there is no other mitred father in the calendar; not Jerome, nor Ambrose, nor Cyril. Thou comest attended with ten thousands of little Loves, and the air is

> Brush'd with the hiss of rustling wings.

Singing Cupids are thy choristers and thy precentors; and instead of the crosier, thy mystical arrow is borne before thee.

In other words, this is the day on which those charming little missives, ycleped Valentines, cross and intercross each other at every street and turning. As the raven himself was hoarse that announced the fatal entrance of Duncan, so the knock of the postman on this day is light, airy, confident, and befitting one that bringeth good tidings. It is less mechanical than on other days; you will say, "That is not the postman, I am sure." Visions of Love, of Cupids, of Hymens!—delightful eternal commonplaces, which, "having been, will always be;" which no schoolboy nor schoolman can write away; having your irreversible throne in the fancy and affections,— what are your transports when the happy maiden, opening with careful finger, not to break the emblematic seal, bursts upon the sight of some well-designed allegory, some youthful fancy, not without verses—

    Lovers, all
    A madrigal,

or some such device, not over-abundant in sense. But all valentines are not foolish. A young man wishing to repay a young maiden for many a favor she had done him, he wrought, unseen and unsuspected, a wondrous work. It was on the finest gilt paper with borders, full, not of common hearts and heartless allegory, but of all the prettiest stories of love from Ovid and older poets than Ovid (he was a scholar). There was Pyramus and Thisbe, and Dido was not forgot, nor Hero and Leander, and swans more than sang in Cayster—in short, a work of magic. This on Valentine's eve he commended to the common post; but the humble medium did its duty, and from his watchful stand, the next morning he saw the cheerful messenger knock; and by and by he saw, unseen, the happy girl unfold the Valentine, dance about, clap her hands, as one after one the pretty emblems unfolded themselves. It was like some fairy present.

Good morrow to my Valentine, sings poor Ophelia
and no better wish, but with better auspices, we wish
to all faithful lovers, who are not too wise to despise
old legends, but are content to rank themselves hum
ble diocesans of old Bishop Valentine.

CHARLES LAMB.

LADY MABEL.

SIDE by side with Lady Mabel
  Sate I, with the sunshade down;
In the distance hummed the Babel
  Of the many-footed town;
There we sate with looks unstable—
  Now of tenderness, of frown.

"Must we part? or may I linger?
  Wax the shadows, wanes the day."
Then, with voice of sweetest singer
  That hath all but died away,
"Go," she said; but tightened finger
  Said articulately, "Stay!"

Face to face with Lady Mabel,
  With the gauzy curtains drawn,
Till a sense I am unable
  To portray, began to dawn;
Till the slant sun flung the gable
  Far athwart the sleepy lawn.

"Now I go. Adieu, adieu love!
  This is weakness; sweet, be strong!

Comes the footfalls of the dew, love!
  Philomel's reminding song."
"Go," she said; "but I go, too, love!
  Go with you, my life long!"

ALFRED AUSTIN.

ST. VALENTINE'S MAGIC WAND.

BEFORE my love and I had met,
  The budding larch was clad with green;
No bitter wind awoke to fret
  The gold locks of the garden's queen;
The chestnut from his kingly throne
  Reigned o'er the dewy lawn, and yet
Their grace they had not wholly shown
  Before my love and I had met.

Before my love and I had met
  The skies were soft as now they be;
The breeze that kissed the violet
  Shook white snow from the hawthorn tree;
With breath of lilacs freshly blown
  My heart was lifted up, and yet
There was a sweetness, all unknown
  Until my love and I had met.

Before my love and I had met,
  The whispers of the pines I heard;
Low warblings paid the shelter-debt
  Where leaves concealed a happy bird;

The river rippled o'er the stone
  The air was thrilled with gladness, yet
Music has gained a deeper tone
    Now that my love and I have met.
                    WILLIAM WATERFIELD.

MEG MAY'S VALENTINE.

OUT of the cottage looked Meg May,
  In the morning light of Valentine's day.

The sun o'er the hills was just in sight,
And the slanting rays of his beams so bright

Lit up Meg's hair like shimmering gold,
As it fell from her temple in careless fold.

She laughed as she saw who was coming that way-
The one she saw first on Valentine's day.

" Old wood-sawing Jim! it is, I declare!
O Jim, you're my Valentine, so beware!"

" I'm glad for mesel', miss, though sorry for you;
But 'tis only the written ones ever come true."

She laughed, and then, warbling a merry lay,
Was soon busy at work in her cheery way—

Dressing the younger boys and girls,
Washing their faces, and twisting their curls;

Telling them when they were ready for school,
To learn all their lessons and keep every rule.

Then she tied back her hair, her soft bright hair,
And fastened a ribbon here and there.

She smoothed the folds of her simple gown
And reached her hood and her mantle down;

Then stopped with an eager yet shameful look,
And fingered the pages of a book,

It does look foolish for me to go
On Valentine's day for a letter I know;

"And yet if I don't, and Roger should write,
'Twill stay there till father comes home to-night.

" Oh! I surely must go! But stay, let me see!
Mother said that she wanted some sugar and tea;

" So I'll go after them, 'tis so pleasant to-day,
And just stop at the office—'tis right on the way."

The hood and the mantle she hastened to don;
Her little white mittens were quickly put on.

All down the street, there's the post-office door,
Just past the corner, a minute more.

"Any letters for me?" in a careless way.
" Your name? Oh! yes! Miss Margaret May."

And into the white-mittened hands
A great white envelope drops. She stands

A moment to read the direction again,
While the rose in her cheek grows redder, and thou

Under her mantle she hides it away.
"I thought he would write me on Valentine's day."

Homeward she hastes; at the garden gate—
"Oh! the sugar and tea! Well, they can wait."

In-doors, up-stairs, in her own little room,
Her cheeks are like the carnation's bloom.

Two doves at the top, and Cupid below;
Two hearts by the arrow shot straight from his bow,

Pierced and transfixed, and verses of love,
With wreaths of bright flowers dropping down
    from above,

And written inside, in the inmost fold,
Was the old-time story so often told.

I think she was satisfied, sweet Meg May,
With the letter that came to her Valentine's day.

VALENTINE TO A MAN OF WORTH.

FAIR Sir! to you my maiden intuitions—
    Shy, but sincere—ingenuously incline,
And if I find you answer the conditions,
    I'll take your bid and be your Valentine.

I know your worth—that is, your general merit;
    But, when your mourned and wealthy father died,
Pray tell a simple girl, did you inherit
    His virtues only—or—a bit beside?

Yes, I admire your lofty reputation,
  Dear to my artless spirit as my own;
But tell me this—to still my trepidation—
  Are you an owner in Bell Telephone?

Your learning, too, has bound my heart in fetters—
  For you are wise, if street report be true;
I, too, a childish fancy have for letters—
  I hope you're solid on "C. B., & Q."

Your noble presence—"dignified and stately"—
  With inexperienced ardor I adore;
But those Villard stocks! Have you tried 'em lately?
  And were you long or short on that Lake Shore?

So, gentle Sir, if you aright but read me,
  And will with all your Bonds and Stocks be mine,
Then into Mutual Union you shall lead me,
  And I will be—
              Your booming VALENTINE.
                    EDWARD A. CHURCH.

IT WAS A LASS.

IT was a lass, for love a-seeking,
  In every heavy red rose peeking—
    Ah, well-a-day!—
To see if there he might be hiding;
And all the while herself a-chiding
For shame, that she desired him so,
And sought him if she would or no.
    Ah, well-a-day!

And when by chance a laddie meeting,
She'd blush, and give him trembling greeting—
    Ah, well-a-day!
And shyly in his eyes be peeping,
To see if Love lay in them sleeping;
And if to wake he 'gan to stir,
And dazzle at the sight of her—
    Ah, well-a-day!

It was a lass, for love a-hunting,
So still, for fear of him affronting—
    Ah, well-a-day!
At last, one eve, with tears and sighing,
She spied him in her own heart lying,
And nowhere else, fore'er and aye—
Ah, well-a-day,
    Ah, well-a-day!

                MARY E. WILKINS.

DIANA'S VALENTINE.

GOOD Saint Valentine, I pray,
   While around this town you stray,
You will keep your eyes alert
For a maid who loves to flirt.

If among the hurrying crowd—
Beauties fair and beauties proud-
You should see one like a queen,

Eyes of blue with golden sheen
In her hair that's flecked with brown,
And a grace about her gown,
That's Diana!

   Catch her eye
As she's gayly tripping by;
Say you know a sorry wight,
Slow of speech and slow to write,
Who would tell her through these flowers
That her eyes are bright as stars
In the blue; that her speech
Haunts his mem'ry (out of reach
Like their perfume faint but fine)
That her laugh is like rare wine.
As you leave her touch her lips;
Say that men are like old ships,
Easy towed, but hard to steer;
Then just whisper in her ear,
Lovers change, but friends are true
Like these violets. Then, "Adieu."

This, Saint Valentine, I pray,
On the morning of that day
When you keep your eyes alert
For all maids who love to flirt.
       ALBERT BRIDGES

PIERROT'S VALENTINE.

HIS loving heart had never learned
    The hopelessness of high ambition,
He thought, poor Pierrot, love could win
    A way to loftiest position.

Nor first nor last of lovers he
    To promise that beyond his art,
Vowing the unattainable
    To win his chosen lady's heart.

"Dear Columbine," he smiling wrote,
    "My valor soars this world above.
I will do that ne'er done before
    That I may win my sweetheart's love

"Above the high cathedral spires
    Hangs the big moon: it shall be thine.
I'll climb and fetch it down to you
    If you will be my valentine."
                  MINNIE BUCHANAN GOODMAN.

ST. VALENTINE'S DAY.

AT morn unto my window sill,
    Dan Cupid comes to learn my will.
"Friend," cries my little naked guest,
"Hast thou for me an amorous quest?

Is there no maid to whom thou'dst say
'I love thee!' on this festal day?"

"Cupid,' I answer, "there's a maid
Of whom my heart is half afraid.
A coward I in lover's bliss—
I'll send, thee, rogue, to steal my kiss!
And take with thee this scarlet rose,
Wherein my love all hotly glows."

Then Cupid thus: "Ho, that will I!
And hid beneath the leaves I'll lie.
When to her room the rose I've borne,
To smell it, sure she'll never scorn;
Then shall I touch her with my dart—
'A bee,' she'll cry, 'is at its heart!'

"The while she standeth startled there,
I shall have vanished in the air;
Then hovering near her lips aflame,
I'll softly whisper her your name,
And of the mystery naught she'll make—
She'll think it was her heart that spake!"

EDWARD VALENTINE.

Washington's Birthday

EULOGY ON WASHINGTON.

AMERICANS! The saviour of your country has obtained his last victory. Having reached the summit of human perfection, he has quitted the region of human glory.

Born to direct the destiny of empires, his character was as majestic as the events, to which it was attached, were illustrious. In the delineation of its features, the vivid pencils of genius cannot brighten a trait, nor the blighting breath of calumny obscure. His principles were the result of organic philosophy,—his success, of moral justice. His integrity assumed the post of command,—his intelligence, the aspect of inspiration. Glory, to many impregnable, he obtained without ambition; popularity, to all inconstant, he enjoyed without jealousy. The one was his from admiration, the other from gratitude. The former embellished, but could not reward; the latter followed, but never could lead him. The robust vigor of his virtue, like the undazzled eye of the eagle, was inaccessible to human weakness; and the unaspiring temperament of his passions, like the regenerating ashes of the phœnix, gave new life to the greatness it could not extinguish. In the imperial dignity of his person was exhibited the august stature of his mind.

ROBERT TREAT PAINE, JR.

WASHINGTON.

ROME had its Cæsar, great and brave; but stain
 was on his wreath;
He lived the heartless conqueror, and died the
 tyrant's death.
France had its eagle; but his wings, though lofty
 they might soar,
Were spread in false ambition's flight, and dipped in
 murder's gore.

Those hero-gods, whose mighty sway would fain
 have chained the waves,
Who flashed their blades with tiger-zeal, to make a
 world of slaves—
Who, though their kindred barred the path, still
 fiercely waded on—
Oh! where shall be their "glory" by the side of
 Washington?

He fought, but not with love of strife—he struck but
 to defend;
And, ere he turned a people's foe, he sought to be a
 friend.
He strove to keep his country's right, by reason's
 gentle word,
And sighed when fell injustice threw the challenge—
 sword to sword.

He stood, the firm, the calm, the wise, the patriot,
 and sage;
He showed no deep, avenging hate—no burst of
 despot rage.

He stood for liberty and truth, and dauntlessly led on,
Till shouts of victory gave forth the name of Washington.

He saved his land, but did not lay his soldier trap-
pings down
To change them for the regal vest, and don a kingly
crown.
Fame was too earnest in her joy—too proud of such
a son—
To let a robe and title mask a noble Washington.
                                    ELIZA COOK.

THE APPROACH OF THE PRESIDENCY.

YOU are among the small number of those who know my invincible attachment to domestic life, and that my sincerest wish is to continue in the enjoyment of it solely until my final hour. But the world would be neither so well instructed, nor so candidly disposed as to believe me uninfluenced by sinister motives, in case my circumstances should render a deviation from the line of conduct I had prescribed to myself indispensable.

Should the contingency you suggest take place, and (for argument's sake alone let me say it) should my unfeigned reluctance to accept the office be overcome by a deference for the reasons and opinions of my friends, might I not, after the declarations I have made (and Heaven knows they were made in the sincerity of my heart), in the judgment of the world and of posterity, be chargeable with levity and inconsistency, if not with rashness and ambition? Nay, further, would there not be some apparent foundation for the two former charges? Now justice to myself and tranquillity of conscience require that I should act a part, if not above imputation, at least capable of vindication. Though I prize as I ought the good opinion of my fellow-citizens, yet, if I know myself, I would not seek or retain popularity at the expense of one social duty or moral virtue.

GEORGE WASHINGTON.

THE FATHER OF HIS COUNTRY.
[Funeral Oration—1800.]

METHINKS I see his august image, and I hear falling from his venerable lips these deep-sinking words:

"Cease, Sons of America, lamenting our separation; go on, and confirm by your wisdom the fruits of our joint councils, joint efforts, and common dangers; reverence religion; diffuse knowledge throughout your land, patronize the arts and sciences; let Liberty and Order be inseparable companions. Control party spirit, the bane of free governments; observe good faith to, and cultivate peace with all nations, shut up every avenue to foreign influence, contract rather than extend national connection, rely on yourselves only: be Americans in thought, word, and deed;

—thus will you give immortality to that union which was the constant object of my terrestrial labors ; thus will you preserve undisturbed to the latest posterity the felicity of a people to me most dear, and thus will you supply (if my happiness is now aught to you) the only vacancy in the round of pure bliss high Heaven bestows."

HENRY LEE.

WASHINGTON'S KISS.

When General Washington visited Andover, Mass., in November, 1789, he breakfasted at the tavern of Deacon Isaac Abbott. As he was leaving, he saw a rip in his glove. He asked Priscilla Abbott, then a young girl, to mend it. Taking it from her when it was finished he gave her a kiss in return.

THRONGED were the streets of Andover town,
  On that morning of long ago,
And swift was the riding up and down,
  And the galloping to and fro.
The judge was there in his stately wig,
  The parson in rustling gown,
And the parish doctor in bran new rig,
  Huzzaed for the brave old town.

" Huzza, huzza, there's the tattered flag
  We carried at Bunker Hill!"
How the old eyes shine, and the old heads wag,
  As over the distant hill,
With drum and fife, and in brave array,
  The scholars of Phillipps' school
Escorted the veterans, old and gray,
  Who had shaken the British rule.

At last in the distance a dusty cloud,
    A sound as of horse's feet,
But they never moved, and they spoke not loud,
    And they heard their own hearts beat.
Then a forward rush, and a mighty cheer,
    And a boom of the Yorktown gun,
As across the plain to their old eyes clear,
    Rode the General—Washington.

He was tall of figure, and grand of face,
    With an eye which was deep and blue,
And an air which told that he came from race
    Who to freedom and God were true.
And they rent the air with their joyful shout
    With their cries of "Welcome—Hail!"
He had cheered them often in storm and rout,
    Unchanged, when their cheeks were pale.

They pressed up close to his bridle rein,
    They touched his extended hand.
He had shared their hunger, their cold, their pain,
    And the strife of their anguished land.
His homeliest wishes for shelter and food
    They served with the tenderest care,
The wise and the simple, the gentle and rude,
    All had in his welcome a share.

Still they served him not upon bended knee,
    As serfs did their lords of yore,
They gave him the homage of men who were free,
    And the love of their heart's deep core.

That he praised our town we nowhere read,
  Though he called Pentucket fair;
And he did not say that in word or deed,
  He thought we were rich or rare.

But he left a token of favoring grace
  To a maiden of Andover town.
A maid who sprang from an ancient race,
  And a name of good renown,
An honored guest in her father's inn,
  He was turning to leave the door,
When he found in his riding glove of tan,
  A rent never seen before.

And looking surprised he caught her smile,
  You knew it, I think he said.
That you will mend it, I am almost sure,
  For you have needle and thread.
Then drawing the glove from his shapely hand
  He watched, as with stitches neat
She fastened together the loosened seam,
  Her fingers—slender and fleet

She finished her task; a little she paused;
  Then handed it with curtsey low;
But, bowing and smiling, he left a kiss
  On her mantling cheek and brow.
Then with flag and drum he was swept away
  To the mansion upon the hill,
And they laughed at the maiden for many a day,
  Because she was grave and still.

'Tis a pleasant tale, and a century now,
  Since the courtly kiss was given.
The maid and the chief in their graves sleep low,
  Their souls we hope are in Heaven.
Nothing 1 know of the maiden's life,
  If she had husband or son.
What matters its joys, its peace, its strife,
  She was kissed by Washington.

PRESIDENT WASHINGTON'S RECEPTIONS.

HE devoted one hour every other Tuesday, from three to four, to these visits. He understood himself to be visited as the "President of the United States," and not on his own account. He was not to be seen by anybody and everybody; but required that every one who came should be introduced by his Secretary, or by some gentleman whom he knew himself. He lived on the south side of Market Street, just below Sixth. The place of reception was the dining-room in the rear, twenty-five or thirty feet in length, including the bow projecting over into the garden. Mrs. Washington received her visitors in the two rooms on the second floor, from front to rear.

At three o'clock, or at any time within a quarter of an hour afterward, the visitor was conducted to this dining-room, from which all seats had been removed for the time. On entering, he saw the tall, manly figure of Washington clad in black velvet; his hair

in full dress, powdered and gathered behind in a
large silk bag; yellow gloves on his hands; holding
a cocked hat with cockade in it, and the edges
adorned with a black feather, about an inch deep.
He wore knee and shoe buckles; and a long sword
with a finely wrought and polished steel hilt. The
scabbard was white polished leather.

He stood always in front of the fireplace, with his
face toward the door of entrance. The visitor was
conducted to him, and he required to have the name
so distinctly pronounced that he could hear it. He
had the very uncommon faculty of associating a
man's name and personal appearance so durably in
his memory, as to be able to call any one by name
who made a second visit. He received his visitor
with a dignified bow, while his hands were so disposed of as to indicate that the salutation was not to
be accompanied with shaking hands. This ceremony
never occurred in these visits, even with his most
near friends, that no distinction might be made.

As these visitors came in, they formed a circle
round the room. At a quarter-past three, the door
was closed, and the circle was formed for that day.
He then began on the right and spoke to each visitor,
calling him by name and exchanging a few words
with him. When he had completed his circuit
he resumed his first position, and the visitors approached him in succession, bowed and retired. By
four o'clock the ceremony was over.

On the evenings Mrs. Washington received visitors,
he did not consider himself as visited. He was then

as a private gentleman, dressed usually in some colored coat and waistcoat, often brown with bright buttons, and black on his lower limbs. He had then neither hat nor sword; he moved about among the company, conversing with one and another. He had once a fortnight an official dinner, and select companies on other days. He sat (it is said) at the side in a central position, Mrs. Washington opposite; the two ends were occupied by members of his family, or by personal friends.

WILLIAM SULLIVAN.

THE BIRTHDAY OF WASHINGTON.

THE birthday of the "Father of his Country!" May it ever be freshly remembered by American hearts! May it ever reawaken in them a filial veneration for his memory; ever rekindle the fires of patriotic regard for the country which he loved so well, to which he gave his youthful vigor and his youthful energy; to which he devoted his life in the maturity of his powers, in the field; to which again he offered the counsels of his wisdom and his experience as president of the convention that framed our Constitution; which he guided and directed while in the chair of state, and for which the last prayer of his earthly supplication was offered up, when it came the moment for him so well, and so grandly, and so calmly, to die. He was the first man of the time in which he grew. His memory is first and most sacred in our love, and ever hereafter, till the last drop of blood shall freeze in the last American heart, his name shall be a spell of power and of might.

Yes, gentlemen, there is one personal, one vast felicity, which no man can share with him. It was the daily beauty and towering and matchless glory of his life which enabled him to create his country, and at the same time secure an undying love and regard from the whole American people. "The first in the hearts of his countrymen!" Yes, first! He has our first and most fervent love. Undoubtedly there were brave and wise and good men before his day, in every colony. But the American nation, as a nation, I do not reckon to have begun before 1774, and the first love of that young America was Washington. The first word she lisped was his name. Her earliest breath spoke it. It still is her proud ejaculation; and it will be the last gasp of her expiring life! Yes; others of our great men have been appreciated—many admired by all—but him we love; him we all love. About and around him we call up no dissentient, discordant, and dissatisfied elements—no sectional prejudice nor bias—no party, no creed, no dogma of politics. None of these shall assail him. Yes; when the storm of battle blows darkest and rages highest, the memory of Washington shall nerve every American arm and cheer every American heart. It shall relume that Promethean fire, that sublime flame of patriotism, that devoted love of country which his words have commended, which his example has consecrated:

" Where may the wearied eye repose,
   When gazing on the great;
 Where neither guilty glory glows
   Nor despicable state?
 Yes—one—the first, the last, the best,
 The Cincinnatus of the West,
   Whom Envy dared not hate,
 Bequeathed the name of Washington.
 To make man blush, there was but one."
                              RUFUS CHOATE.

EASTER

THE FLOWER'S EASTER MESSAGE

FRESH hope and cheer
    By symbol clear
The flowers brings us, year by year.

    They bloom, they fall,
    They slumber all;
The brown earth is their funeral pall;

    But lo! some day
    Along our way,
They live again, as sweet and gay;

    For earth's dark tomb
    But hid in gloom
The life that now doth newly bloom.

    Oh! then repeat
    Your message sweet,
Dear flowers, blooming at our feet;

    And this new spring
    Help us to fling
Aside our doubt and wondering;

    To hope and trust
    That all life must,
Like yours, be rescued from the dust.

EMILIE POULSSON.

MARY AT THE SEPULCHRE.

'THEN, while the first day of the week was dark,
  Alone I wended to the sepulchre,
Bearing fair water, and the frankincense,
And linen, that my Lord's sweet body sleep
Well in the rock. And while my woeful feet
Passed through the gate, and up the paved ascent
Along the second wall, over the hill,
Into that garden, hard by Golgotha,
The morning brightened over Moab's peaks,
Touched the great temple's dome with crimson fires,
Lit Ophel and Moriah rosy-red,
Made Olivet all gold, and, in the pools
In Hinnom laid a sudden lance of flame,
And, from the thorn-trees, brake the waking songs
Of little birds; and every palm-tree's top
Was full of doves that cooed, as knowing not
How Love was dead, and Life's dear glory gone,
And the world's hope lay in the tomb with Him;
Which now I spied—that hollow in the rock
Under the camphire leaves. Yet, no guards there
To help me roll away the stone! nay, and no stone!
It lay apart, leaving the door a-gape,
And through the door, as I might dimly see,
The scattered wrappings of the burial-night.
I sped; and came to Peter, and to John;
And cried: 'Our Lord is stolen from His grave
And none to tell where He is borne away!'
Thereat, they ran together, came, and saw
And entered in; and found the linen-cloths

Scattered; the rock-bed empty; and, amazed,
Back to their house they went. But I drew nigh
A second time, alone; heart-broken now,
The bright day seeming blackest night to me.
Why should earth wake, the Son of Man asleep?
Fled, too, my last fond hope, to lay Him fair,
And kiss His wounded feet, and wash the blood
From the pierced palms, and comb His tangled hair
To comeliness, and leave Him—like a King—
To His forgetful angels. Weeping hard
With these thoughts, like to snake-fangs stinging me
My left hand on the stone I laid, and shut
The eager sunshine off with my right hand,
Kneeling, and looking in the sepulchre.
It was not dark within! I deemed at first
A lamp burned there, such radiance mild I saw
Lighting the hewn walls, and the linen bands;
And, in one corner, folded by itself,
The face-cloth. Coming closer, I espied
Two men who sate there—very watchfully—
One at the head, the other at the foot
Of that stone table where my Lord had lain.
Oh! I say, 'men'—I should have known no men
Had eyes like theirs, shapes so majestical,
Tongues turned to such a music as the tone
Wherewith they questioned me: 'Why weepest thou?'
'Ah, sirs!' I said, 'My Lord is ta'en away,
Nor wot we whither!' and thereat my tears
Blotted all seeing. So, I turned to wipe
The hot drops off; and, look! another one
Standing behind me, and my foolish eyes
Hard gazing on Him, and not knowing Him!

Indeed, I deemed this was the gardener;
Albeit, if I had marked—such light
Of loveliest compassion in His face,
Had told my beating heart and blinded eyes
WHO this must be. But I—my brow i' the dust—
Heard him say softly: 'Wherefore weepest thou?
Whom seekest thou?' A little marvelled I—
Still at His foot, too sorrowful to rise—
He should ask this, the void grave gaping near;
Nathless, not lifting up my foolish head,
'Sir,' said I, 'if 'tis thou hast borne Him hence,
Tell me where thou hast laid Him. Then will I bear
    Him away!'"
               "What answer came to that?"
"Ah, friend, such answer that my sadness turned
Gladness, as suddenly as gray is gold
When the sun springs in glory! A dear word
Spoke first to me, and, after me, to all,
That all may always know He is the Lord,
And Death is dead, and new times come to men;
And Heaven's ways justified, and Christ alive,
Whom we saw die, nailed on the cruel cross!
For, while I lay there, sobbing at His feet,
The word He spake—My Lord! my King! my Christ!
Was my name:
      'MARY!'
          No language had I then,
No language have I now! only I turned
My quick glance upward; saw Him; knew Him!
    sprang
Crying: 'Rabboni!—Lord! my Lord! dear Lord!'"
                      SIR EDWIN ARNOLD.

PEACE.

ERE our dear Saviour spoke the parting word
   To those who loved Him best when here below,
While deep emotion every bosom stirred,
   He said, " My peace I give you ere I go!"

His Peace, sweet Peace! As falls the summer dew
   On drooping flowers, so fell those words of cheer
Upon the earnest hearts that dimly knew
   What they, like their dear Lord, must suffer here.

His Peace—Christ's Peace! O gift most rare and strange!
   Never was aught so precious given before!
Vain trifler he who would that gift exchange
   For all the riches of Golconda's shore!

His Peace—His blessed Peace! Not Joy, the bright,
   Bewildering sprite that charmed their early years,
When with youth's roses crowned, and clad in light,
   Her radiant eyes had ne'er been dimm'd by tears,—

But Peace that walks with Patience, side by side,
   Bearing Heaven's seal upon her pure, calm face;
Child of Submission, whatsoe'er betide,
   She wears the white robes of celestial grace.

O Christ! whose human heart remembers still
   The pangs from which death only gave release,
Strange griefs, strange fears, our yearning souls must fill,
   Withhold what else thou wilt—but give us Peace!
                        JULIA C. R. DORR.

THE EASTER ALTAR-CLOTH.

SOLEMN days of Lent are closing, and in soft
 ethereal light
Earth and sky delay, transfigured, at the sepulchre
 of night,
While reluctant steal the shadows o'er the smoothly-
 burnished sea,
Loth to gloom the shining pageant with their purple mystery.

Yonder, where the misty sunlight on that distant
 city falls,
Stands a convent, dark and stately, rearing high its
 ancient walls.
Long ago—so runs the story—at this very day and
 hour,
Wan and pale a nun was sitting in that topmost
 gloomy tower.

On her lap were folds of beauty, broidered with the
 finest art,
Gleaming with the sacred symbols she had wrought
 so long apart;
And the fabric's dazzling whiteness, marvelous in
 leaf and line,
Seemed a snowdrift frosted over with each emblematic sign.

Ah, how many years in secret she had labored, day
 by day,

That some happy Easter morning she might on the
  altar lay
There at last her precious treasure, as an offering to
  her Lord,
With each thread a prayer inwoven answering to His
  holy Word.

Now her task is almost ended; all but finished there
  it lies!
In and out the needle glances—fast, and faster still
  it flies—
While the last rich beams of sunset o'er the dusky
  gloaming come,
Flinging bars of golden glory in the narrow, sombre
  room.

In those wondrous lights and shadows Rembrandt
  loved to paint so well
Like a patron-saint of Labor there she sits—but list!
  a bell
Strikes upon the breathless silence, and she starts up
  cold and white,
" Yet again, and must I leave thee! Oh! I cannot go
  to-night!

"I must stay my dream to finish; some one else can
  do I know
Just as well my every duty if for once I do not go.
Peace! begone, temptations evil! longer here 1 must
  not stay "—
And she crossed herself and sadly laid the glistening
  cloth away.

Clad in mournful sable habit through the doorway
see her glide,
Through the corridors, as silent, through the arching
portals wide;
Out across the court deserted, till, at length, she gains
the street,
Mingles with the throng, nor pauses till her tired
aching feet

Reach the hospital that rises just outside the city's
wall,
Where its dark, funereal shadow on the landscape
throws a pall.
Safe at last within its shelter from the tempter's
dreaded claim,
Dying eyes are watching for her, dying murmurs
speak her name.

Here she sits beside a pallet, reading words of cheer,
and there
Kneels and wafts a soul to heaven on the faithful
wings of prayer,
Thus employed with ceaseless mission night anon has
worn away,
And the starry hosts have vanished through the
glowing arch of day.

Like another fleeting shadow, does the gentle sister
seem,
As she steals back to the convent in the morning's
early gleam.

And a thousand silver voices ring out on the Easter
    air
As she enters through the doorway, climbs again the
    winding stair.

She has reached the cell so dreary where she sees
    with saddest heart
Snowy cloth outspread before her—but what means
    that sudden start?
Lo! in perfect beauty, finished there each vine, each
    symbol lies—
Who has guessed her guarded secret? Who pre-
    pared this strange surprise?

While she stands, perplexed with wonder, see, a
    brightness floods the room,
Greater than the noontide's splendor, rarer than the
    dawning's bloom.
Prostrate low before the vision, thrilled with love, she
    knows full well
Only pitying hands of angels could have wrought
    that miracle.

JULIA H. THAYER.

THE MIRACLE OF THE ROSES.

THERE dwelt in Bethlehem a Jewish maid,
    And Zillah was her name; so passing fair
That all Judea spake the virgin's praise.
He who had seen her eye's dark radiance,
How it revealed her soul, and what a soul!

Beamed in the mild effulgence, woe to him!
For not in solitude, for not in crowds,
Might he escape remembrance, nor avoid
Her imaged form which followed everywhere,
And filled the heart and fixed the absent gaze.
Alas for him! her bosom owned no love
Save the strong ardor of religious zeal;
For Zillah upon heaven had centred all
Her spirit's deep affections. So for her
Her tribesmen sighed in vain, yet reverenced
The firm resolve that destroyed their hopes.

One man there was, a vain and wretched man,
Who saw, desired, despaired, and hated her.
She loathed the man, for Hamuel's eye was bold,
And the strong workings of brute selfishness
Had molded his broad features; and she
Feared the bitterness of wounded vanity.
Nor vain her fear, for Hamuel vowed revenge,
And laid a plot against her spotless fame.
He spread abroad whispers and ill reports
That soon obtained belief; how Zillah's eye,
When, in the temple, heavenward it was raised,
Did swim with rapturous zeal, but there were those
Who had beheld the enthusiast's melting glance
With other feelings filled; that Zillah's life was evil.
Yea, and should be forfeit to the law.
Shame, shame to man that he should trust
The tongue that stabs another's fame!
The ill-report was heard, repeated, and believed,
And soon, for Hamuel, by his well-schemed villainy,

Produced such semblances of guilt,
The maid was to the fire condemned.

Without the wall there was a barren field,
A place abhorred; for there wretched criminals
Received their doom! There they fixed the stake,
And piled the fuel round the injured maid,
Abandoned, as it seemed, by God and man.
The assembled Bethlehemites beheld the scene,
And when they saw the maid bound to the stake.
With what calm holiness she lifted up
Her patient looks to heaven, they doubted her guilt.
With other thoughts stood Hamuel near the pile;
Savage joy had led him thitherward.
But now within his heart unwonted feelings stirred,
And the first pangs of awakening guilt.
The eye of Zillah fell on the slanderer once,
And rested on him for a moment:
Like a dagger it pierc'd and struck into his soul.
Conscience! thou God within us! Not in the hour
Of triumph dost THOU spare the guilty wretch;
Not in the hour of infamy and death
Forsake the faithful! They draw near the stake—
They bring the torch—hold! hold your erring hands!
Yet quench the rising flames! they rise! they spread!
They reach the suffering maid. O God! protect
The innocent one!

They rose, they spread, they raged;
The breath of God went forth: the ascending **fire**
Beneath its influence bent, and all its flames

In one long lightning flash concentrating,
Darted and blasted Hamuel—him alone!

  * * * * * *

Hark! what a fearful scream the multitude
Pour forth! And yet more miracles! the stake
Branches and buds, and spreading its green leaves,
Embowers and canopies the innocent maid,
Who there stands glorified; and roses, then,
First seen on earth since Paradise was lost,
Profusely bloom around her, white and red,
In all their rich variety of hues;
And fragrance, such as our first parents breathed
In Eden, she inhales, vouchsafed to her
A presage sure of Paradise regained!

ROBERT SOUTHEY

O CHRIST, OUR KING.

O BABE of Bethlehem, I pause to hear
 The angel voices chiming sweet and clear;
I lift my eyes to seek the wondrous star
That led the wise men from their home afar;
I bend with them in humblest awe to see
The Kingly One who sat on Mary's knee!
The lowly, meek, yet royal One, who bore
The burden of the cross till life was o'er.
O Christ, our King, half mortal, all divine,
Who e'er can comprehend such love as thine?

BACK AGAIN!

THE chill snows lingered, the spring was late,
It seemed a weariful while to wait
For warmth, and fragrance, and song, and flowers.
And balmy airs and delicious showers.

But we bided our time, and with patient eyes
We watched the slowly relenting skies,
Till at last one April morning we woke
To find we were free of the winter's yoke,

And a rush of wings through the rushing rain
Told us the birds were back again.
A joyous tumult we heard aloft—
Clear, rippling music and fluttering soft.

So light of heart and so light of wing,
All hope of summer, delight of spring,
They seemed to utter with voices sweet,
Upborne on their airy pinions fleet.

Dainty, delicate, lovely things!
Would that my thoughts, like you, had wings
To match your grace, your charm, your cheer,
Your fine, melodious atmosphere!

Precious and beautiful gifts of God,
Scattered through heaven and earth abroad!
Who, ungrateful, would do you wrong,
Check your flight and your golden song?

O friendly spirits! O sweet, sweet birds!
Would I could put my welcome in words
Fit for such singers as you to hear,
Sky-born minstrels and poets dear!

CELIA THAXTER.

IN THE BREAKING OF THE DAY.

IN the gray of Easter even,
   When the light begins to fade,
Fly two angels out of heaven,
   Veiled in vesper shade.
And they watch by those who sleep,
   As they watch Immanuel's rest,
And they comfort all who weep,
   As they soothed sad Mary's breast.
Soft they whisper through the night,
"Wait until the morning light!
From your sorrow look away
To the breaking of the day!"

In the Easter dawn victorious,
   When the stars in rose-light fade,
Rise those angels plumed and glorious,
   Like the sun arrayed.
And they gather up the flowers
   From the purple plains of morning,
Far and wide in bloomy showers,
   Graves of midnight woe adorning—

Saying, singing, " Christ is risen!
Watch no more the open prison;
He has led your loved away
In the breaking of the day!"

FRANCIS L. MACE.

THE DREAM THAT CAME TRUE.

A NIGH a frozen mere a cottage stood,
   A piercing wind swept round and shook the door,
The shrunken door, an easy way made good,
   And drove long drifts of snow along the floor.
It sparkled there like diamonds, for the moon
Was shining in, and night was at the noon.

Before her dying embers, bent and pale,
   A woman sat because her bed was cold;
She heard the wind, the driving sleet and hail,
   And she was hunger-bitten, weak, and old;
Yet while she cowered, and while the casement shook,
Upon her trembling knees she held a book.

A comfortable book to them that mourn,
   And good to raise the courage of the poor;
It lifts the veil and shows beyond the bourne,
   Their Elder Brother, from His home secure,
That for them desolate He died to win,
Repeating, " Come, ye blessed, enter in."

What thought she on, this woman? On her days
   Of toil, or on the supperless night forlorn?

I think not so; the heart but seldom weighs
  With conscious care a burden always borne;
And she was used to these things, had grown old
In fellowship with toil, hunger, and cold.

Then did she think how sad it was to live
  Of all the good this world can yield bereft?
No, her untutored thoughts she did not give
  To such a theme; but in their warp and weft
She wove a prayer; then in the midnight deep
Faintly and slow she fell away to sleep.

A strange, a marvelous sleep, which brought a dream,
  And it was this: that all at once she heard
The pleasant babbling of a little stream
  That ran beside her door, and then a bird
Broke out in song. She looked, and lo! the rime
And snow had melted; it was summer time!

She said, "I will betake me to my door,
  And will look out and see this wondrous sight,
How summer is come back, and frost is o'er,
  And all the air warm waxen in a night."
With that she opened, but for fear she cried,
For lo! two angels—one on either side.

And while she looked, with marveling measureless,
  The angels stood conversing face to face,
But neither spoke to her. "The wilderness,"
  One angel said, "that solitary place,
Shall yet be glad for Him." And then full fain
The other angel answered, "He shall reign."

And when the woman heard, in wondering wise,
   She whispered, "They are speaking of my Lord."
And straightway swept across the open skies
   Multitudes like to these. They took the word,
That flock of angels, "He shall come again,
My Lord, my Lord!" they sang, "and He shall reign."

Then they, drawn up into the blue o'erhead,
   Right happy, shining ones, made haste to flee;
And those before her, one to other said,
   "Behold He stands beneath yon almond tree."
This when the woman heard, she fain had gazed,
But paused for reverence, and bowed down amazed.

After she looked, for this her dream was deep;
   She looked and there was naught beneath the tree;
Yet did her love and longing overleap
   The fear of angels, awful though they be,
And she passed out between the blessed things,
And brushed her mortal weeds against their wings.

Oh! all the happy world was in its best;
   The trees were covered thick with buds and flowers,
And these were dropping honey; for the rest,
   Sweetly the birds were piping in their bowers;
Across the grass did groups of angels go,
And saints in pairs were walking to and fro.

Then did she pass toward the almond tree,
   And none she saw beneath it; yet each saint
Upon his coming meekly bent the knee,
   And all their glory as they gazed waxed faint.

And then a 'lighting angel neared the place,
And folded his fair wings before his face.

She also knelt and spread her aged hands,
  As feeling for the sacred human feet;
She said, "Mine eyes are held, but if He stands
  Anear, I will not let Him hence retreat
Except He bless me." Then, O sweet! O fair!
Some words were spoken, but she knew not where.

She knew not if beneath the boughs they woke,
  Or dropt upon her from the realms above,
"What wilt thou, woman?" in the dream He spoke
  "Thy sorrow moveth me, thyself I love;
Long have I counted up thy mournful years;
Once I did weep to wipe away thy tears."

She said, "My one Redeemer, only blest,
  I know Thy voice, and from my yearning heart
Draw out my deep desire, my great request,
  My prayer, that I might enter where Thou art.
Call me, O call from this world troublesome,
And let me see Thy face." He answered, "Come."
                                JEAN INGELOW.

A LEGEND OF THE ASPEN.

WHAT whispers so strange at the hour of midnight,
  From the aspen's leaves trembling so wildly?
Why in the lone wood sings it sad, when the bright
  Full moon beams upon it so mildly?

It soundeth as 'mid the harp-strings the wind-gust,
　　Or like sighs of ghosts wandering in sorrow
In the meadow the small flowers hear it, and must
　　With tears close themselves till the morrow.

"O tell me, poor wretch, why thou shiverest so,—
　　Why the moans of distraction thou pourest;
Say can thy heart harbor repentance and woe?
　　Can sin reach the child of the forest?"

"Yes," sighed forth the tremulous voice,—"for thy race
　　Has not alone fallen from its station;
Not alone art thou seeking for comfort and grace,
　　Nor alone art thou called to salvation.

"I've heard, too, the voice, which, with heaven reconciled,
　　The earth to destruction devoted;
But the storm from my happiness hurried me wild,
　　Though round me joy's melodies floated.

"By Kedron I stood, and the bright beaming eye
　　I viewed of the pitying Power;
Each tree bowed its head, as the Saviour passed by,
　　But I deigned not my proud head to lower.

"I towered to the cloud, whilst the lilies sang sweet,
　　And the rose bent its stems in devotion;
I strewed not my leaves 'fore the Holy One's feet,
　　Nor bough nor twig set I in motion.

"Then sounded a sigh from the Saviour's breast;
　　And I quaked, for that sigh through me darted:

Quake so till I come!' said the voice of the Blest;
   My repose then forever departed.

" And now must I tremble by night and by day,
   For me there no moment of ease is;
I must sigh with regret in such dolorous way,
   While each flow'ret can smile when it pleases.

" And tremble shall I till the last day arrive,
   And I view the Redeemer returning;
My sorrow and punishment long will survive,
   Till the world shall in wild flames be burning."

So whispers the doomed one at midnight; its tone
   Is that of ghosts wandering in sorrow;
The small flowers hear it within the wood lone,
   And with tears close themselves till the morrow,
            BERNHARD SEVERIN INGEMANN.

THE BLIND COMMUNICANT.

THE Saviour's feast was spread. Group after
   group
From Zion's scattering band now silent thronged
Around the sacred table, glad to pay,
As far as sinful, erring man can pay,
Their debt of gratitude, and share anew
The plain memorials of His dying love.
All ranks were gathered there. The rich and poor,
The ignorant and wise; the tear-wet soul,
And the glad spirit yet in sunshine clad.
All, with their many hopes and cares and griefs,

Sought quiet and unmarked their 'customed place;
And still at the full banquet there was room.
It was a solemn season, and I sat.
Wrapped in a cloud of thought, until a slow
And measured footstep fell upon my ear;
And when I turned to look, an aged man
Of three-score years and ten appeared to view.
It was the blind communicant. He came
Led by a friendly hand, and took his place
Nearest the table with a reverent air;
As if he felt the spot was holy ground.
There was a perfect hush: the hour was come;
The symbols were disclosed, and soon there rose
The sweet tones of the shepherd of the flock,
Telling once more the story of the cross;
And as he spoke, in sympathy I gazed
Upon the blind old pilgrim by my side.
The sight was touching. As the pastor taught
In accents all subdued, how Jesus bore
The flight of friends, the stern denial-vow,
The spear, the thorns, the agonizing cross,
With want, shame, persecution, torture, death,
The old man shook, convulsed; a few big tears
Ran trickling down his cheek, and from his lip
Methought there came the words, "Lord is it I?"
But when there stole upon each listening ear
And throbbing heart that prayer of matchless love,
That type and watchword for all after-prayer,
"Father, forgive them!"—then he clasped his hands,
And, bowing his hoary head upon his breast,
Wept even as a gentle child might weep.

There was a change. The bread and wine were
    brought.
He wiped the gushing drops from his thin cheek,
Bowed solemnly; received them both, then paused;
Till, raising his dull eyeballs up to heaven,
As asking for God's blessing on the rite,
He broke the bread, received the goblet close
Within his withered hands; restored it safe;
Then, while a peaceful smile illumed his face,
Sank back as in an ecstasy of bliss.
The parting hymn was sung, and oft I paused
And loved to listen as the old man's voice,
Broken and shrill, sought too to mingle in
With modulated tones; and though his lip
Uttered no music, yet I joyed to know
The heart was linkéd melody within.
Christ's seal was stamped anew upon each soul;
The solemn rite was finished, and the band,
Moved full of thoughtful cheerfulness along
The quiet churchyard, where gay sunbeams danced
On the white marble tombs, and bright flowers made
A pleasant home for Death; while 'mongst them all
The blind communicant went groping on
Along his midnight path. The sight was sad;
My heart yearned for him, and I longed for power
To say as the disciples said of old,
"Blind man, receive thy sight!" And in the might
Of strong compassion I could even, methought,
Have entered his dark prison-house awhile,
And let him gaze in turn on the blue skies
And the glad sunshine and the laughing earth.

But soon I gained a sense of higher things,
And in the heart's soft dialect I said:
"Old soldier of the cross, 'tis well with thee;
Thy warfare is nigh finished; and though earth
Be but an utter blank, yet soon thou'lt gaze
On that bright country where thy God shall be
The never-setting sun; and Christ, thy Lord,
Will lead thee through green pastures where the soil
And living waters play. And though thou art
A creature lonely and unprized by men,
Yet thou may'st stand a prince 'mongst princes when
The King makes up His jewels."

MARY E. LEE.

THE CROWN.

THE crowns of earth are jewelled dust
    Or weights, the wearer's brow to press;
But Thou, O Christ! dost give the just
    A nobler crown of righteousness.

That crown, of Thine own love the seal,
    On Thine a gift of love bestowed,
Diviner splendors shall reveal
    Than e'er on princely head have glowed.

Ten thousand faithful souls and true
    Now wear the crown that wore Thy shame,
That many a wasting anguish knew,
    And as through fire to glory came.

We yet must wage the long-drawn strife,
   And oft with prayers our groans ascend;
We battle for immortal life—
   Give strength and courage to the end.

Then be it ours to hear Thee say,
   When we shall lay our armor down,—
"The faith ye kept! Ye won the day!
   Come, take and wear the matchless crown!"
RAY PALMER.

ARBOR DAY

SPRING.

THE first sparrow of Spring! The year beginning with younger hope than ever! The faint silvery warblings heard over the partially bare and moist fields from the blue-bird, the song-sparrow, and the red-wing, as if the last flakes of winter twinkled as they fell! What at such a time are histories, chronologies, traditions, and all written revelations? The brooks sing carols and glees to the spring. The marsh-hawk sailing low over the meadow is already seeking the first oozy life that awakes. The sinking sound of melting snow is heard in all dells, and the ice dissolves apace in the ponds. The grass flames up on the hillsides like a spring fire,—as if the earth sent forth an inward heat to greet the returning sun; not yellow but green is the color of its flame; the symbol of perpetual youth, the grass-blade, like a long green ribbon, streams from the sod into the summer, checked indeed by the frost, but anon pushing on again, lifting its spear of last year's hay with the fresh life below.

I hear a song-sparrow singing,—"olit, olit, olit, chip, chip, chip, che, char,—che-wiss, che-wiss, wiss, wiss. The pitch-pines and shrub-oaks which had so long

drooped, suddenly resumed their several characters,
looked brighter, greener, and more erect and alive,
after the spring rain. And so the season went rolling on into summer, as one rambles into higher and
higher grass; till anon the oaks, hickorics, maples,
and other trees, putting out amid the pine-woods,
imparted a brightness like sunshine to the landscape.

HENRY DAVID THOREAU.

THREE TREES.

THE pine-tree grew in the wood,
    Tapering, straight, and high;
Stately and proud it stood,
    Black-green against the sky.
Crowded so close, it sought the blue,
And ever upward it reached and grew.

The oak-tree stood in the field,
    Beneath it dozed the herds;
It gave to the mower a shield,
    It gave a home to the birds.
Sturdy and broad, it guarded the farms,
With its brawny trunk and knotted arms.

The apple-tree grew by the wall,
    Ugly and crooked and black;
But it knew the gardener's call,
    And the children rode on its back.
It scattered its blossoms upon the air,
It covered the ground with fruitage fair.

"Now, hey," said the pine, "for the **wood!**
    Come, live with the forest-band,
  Our comrades will do you good,
    And tall and straight you will stand."
  And he swung his boughs to a witching **sound**,
  And flung his cones like coins around.

"Oho!" laughed the sturdy oak,
  "The life of the field for me,
I weather the lightning stroke;
  My branches are broad and free.
Grow straight and slim in the wood, if you will
Give me the sun and a wind-swept hill."

And the apple-tree murmured low;
  "I am neither straight nor strong
Crooked my back does grow
  With bearing my burdens long."
And it dropped its fruit as it dropped a tear,
And reddened the ground with fragrant cheer.

And the Lord of the Harvest heard
  And He said: "I use them all;
For the bough that shelters a bird,
  For the beam that pillars a hall;
And grow they tall, or grow they ill,
They grow but to wait their Master's **will."**

For a ship of oak was sent
  Far over the ocean blue,
And the pine was the mast that **bent**
  As over the waters they flew,
And the ruddy fruit of the apple-**tree**
Was borne to a starving isle of the sea.

Now the farmer grows like the oak,
  And the townsman is proud and tall,
And the city and field are full of folk
  But the Lord has need of them all.
And who will be like the apple-tree
That fed the starving over the sea?
                    CHARLES H. CRANDALL

SPRING.

JUST a tiny blue-eyed maid,
  Newly out of Eden strayed;
Lips, a bud rose-tinted, rare,
And the sunlight in her hair—
    Here is Spring!

Leaves are few to make her bowers,
Bunches bright of leafless flowers
Are by baby fingers placed
Side by side in happy haste—
    Little Spring!

Gardens dark with winter gloom,
All at once begin to bloom;
Budding branches, lifted high,
Laugh and whisper in the sky,
    " Welcome Spring!"

She will reach their stately height
What to her are blossoms bright?
Little Spring, in haste to pass,

>   Lets them fall among the grass—
>   Eager Spring!
>
> Tiptoe stands, with parted lips,
> Cannot reach their swaying tips,
> Brushes past in April grief—
> See! The underwood in leaf!
>   Fairy Spring!
>
> She is growing tall and slim,
> And her eyes are darkly dim,
> Deepening with the deepening sky,
> Darkening with the bluebell's dye—
>   Is it Spring?
>
> They were wide and undismayed,
> Timid now, and veiled in shade;
> Comes a sound of hurrying feet,
> She is flushed with roses sweet—
>   Happy Spring!

MARGARET VELEY

PLANTING THE OAK.

> IN mellowing skies the mated robins sing,
>   The west winds blow the flag of clustered stars,
> And showers of roses waft the skies of spring
>   O'er bloodless fields and monuments of wars.
> The waters purling flow the green woods through,
>   The hermit moons ascend the glimmering sea.

Peaceful, as when war's silver trumpets blew
  A Truce of God or pastoral jubilee.

Here, as we gather on this festal day,
  To plant the acorn, heir of centuries old,
The oak of warrior kings and courtiers gay,
  Of airy Dryads and the age of gold,
What war scenes rise—what navies dark and grand,
  With peaking oars and serried shields and bows,
What Roman roads with bannered eagles spanned,
  And cooled with shades of pendant mistletoes!

O acorn, acorn! Fancy sees again
  Manorial halls and forests cool and broad,
Where villeins cluster 'mid the rosy rain
  Of darkening sunsets 'round the feudal lord;
Sees the rude arkwrights with their trenchers white,
  Old Norman barons, knights of gay Gascogne,
And palgraves tall with battle axes bright,
  And marching palmers—gone, forever gone!

I hear grand Nelson's cry—"Strike, hearts of oak!"
  And see the smitten Dane-ships strew the shore,
And, from the Baltic roll the battle smoke
  O'er deep sea graves of mourning Elsinore;
Before the oaks I see Gibraltar fall,
  And Trafalgar, and from the Tagus sweep
The Genoese on oak-ribbed caravel
  To pluck the golden empires of the deep.

O oaks of eld, where wandered kirtled maids,
  When swung the orioles in the sunlit rain,

I see ye gathered for the palisades,
  From which gonfalon never yet was ta'en;
I see your trunks, once spun with gossamers,
  Where fanchons sung, in rows defiant rise,
And cavaliers, with golden stars of spurs,
  Their shelter seek, with battle-weary eyes!

Mother of cradles, where the infant dreams!
  Father of ships, that thunder on the sea!
The soldier's lance, above whose steel tongue gleams
  Or Cross, or Crescent, or the Fleur-de-lis!
Couch of the victor, who no more shall wake!
  The dead king's throne, when, 'mid the hush of prayers.
The dark lords pass, their last quick look to take,
  The mullioned windows toward the altar stairs.

We plant the acorn—open here the mold,
  The violets break while thrushes flute and sing,
Earth's new-made vesture let the spade unfold—
  We plant the acorn in the breath of spring,
The sun will find it, and the April rain,
  The jocund June, and summer's wandering wind
Life's resurrected powers renew again
  The embryo oak, and nature's chain unbind.

Like her, the maid of far Mauritius' palms,
  Virginia, in Provence tale of love,
Whose simple history still the worn world charms,
  Who 'mid the citron shades was wont to rove.
And tamarinds cool, and fans of cocoanuts gay,
  And planted there a seed in gratitude

For every fruit she tasted—so, to-day,
  We plant the acorn, grateful for the wood.

Rise, acorn, rise, the south wind's breath shall blow
  Among thy lobed and sinuated leaves,
As in the Vosges where the child-oaks grow,
  Or Javan valleys where the sea wind breathes,
The showers thy buds, regenerate, shall baptize,
  And earth shall feed thee like a mother strong,
Heir of the sun, the cloud, the eternal skies,
  And earth's new ages, eloquent and long.

The heir of peace—the dove descends and falls
  From Christ's own hand upon young Freedom's brow;
We weave the garlands of new festivals,
  Like poets old, to lay upon the plough.
No more for dragon-ship, or palisade
  The young tree rises by the crumbling wood,
But children plant the royal oaks to shade
  The councils sweet of human brotherhood!

            HEZEKIAH BUTTERWORTH.

WEST WIND.

Translated by Sir Edwin Arnold.

COME forth, all ye blossoms!
  Start, seeds, from the land;
Ye songs of birds, waken,
  I, Spring, am at hand.

My touch on the fir-boughs,
  My kiss in the air,
Makes odors of heaven
  Spread sweet everywhere.

And the fragrance and splendor
  Of meadow and grove
I give for a bride-wreath
  In free gift to Love.

Come forth, then, blue violets!
  Spring calleth on you;
Wake, leaflets and flow'rets,
  For love's coming too.

                CARMEN SYLVA.

HEARD YE O' THE TREE O' LIBERTY?

UPO' this tree there grows sic fruit,
  Its virtues a' can tell, man;
It raises men aboon the brute,
  It makes him ken himsel', man.
Gif ance the peasant taste a bit,
  He's greater than a lord, man,
And wi' the beggar shares a mite
  O' a' he can afford, man.

This fruit is worth a' Afric's wealth,
  To comfort us 'twas sent, man;
To gie the sweetest blush o' health,
  And mak' us a' content, man;

It clears the een, it cheers the heart,
  Maks high and low guid friends, **man;**
And he wha acts the traitor's part,
  It to perdition sends, man.

My blessings aye attend the chiel,
  Wha pitied Gallia's slaves, man,
And slaw a branch, spite o' the deil,
  Fra yont the western waves, man.
Fair Virtue watered it wi' care,
  And now she sees wi' pride, man,
How weel it buds and blossoms there,
  Its branches spreading wide, man.

But vicious folk aye hate to see
  The works o' virtue thrive, man.
The courtly vermin's banned the **tree,**
  And grat to see it thrive, man.
King Loui thought to cut it down,
  When it was unco' sma', man;
For this the watchman cracked his **crown,**
  Cut aff his head and a', man.

A wicked crew syne, on a time,
  Did take a solemn aith, man,
It ne'er should flourish to its prime,
  I wat they pledged their faith, **man.**
Awa' they gazed wi' mock parade,
  Like beagles hunting game, man,
But soon grew weary o' the trade,
  And wished they'd been at hame, **man.**

For Freedom, standing by the tree,
  Her sons did loudly ca', man;
She sang a sang o' liberty,
  Which pleased them ane and a', man.
By her inspired, the new-born race
  Soon drew the avenging steel, man;
The hirelings ran—her foes gied chase,
  And banged the despot weel, man,

Wi' plenty o' sic trees, I trow,
  The warld would live in peace, man;
The sword would help to mak a plough,
  The din o' war wad cease, man.
Like brethren in a common cause,
  We'd on each other smile, man;
And equal rights and equal laws
  Wad gladden each and all, man.

Wae worth the loon wha wadna eat
  Sic halesome dainty cheer, man;
I'd gie my shoon frae off my feet,
  To taste sic fruit, I swear, man.
Syne let us pray ev'ry land may
  Sure plant this far-famed tree, man;
And blithe we'll sing, and hail the day
  That shone on Liberty's tree, man.

ROBERT BURNS.

THE LAUREL-SEED.

A DESPOT gazed on sun-set clouds,
   Then sank to sleep amidst the gleam;—
Forthwith, a myriad starving slaves
   Must realize his lofty dream.

Year upon year, all night and day,
   They toiled, they died,—and were replaced;
At length, a marble fabric rose
   With cloud-like domes and turrets graced.

No anguish of those herds of slaves
   E'er shook one dome or wall asunder,
Nor wars of other mighty kings,
   Nor lustrous javelins of the thunder.

One sunny morn a lonely bird,
   Pass'd o'er, and dropt a laurel-seed;
The plant sprang up amidst the walls
   Whose chinks were full of moss and weed.

The laurel-tree grew large and strong,
   Its roots went searching deeply down;
It split the marble walls of Wrong,
   And blossom'd o'er the Despot's crown.

And in its boughs a nightingale
   Sings to those world-forgotten graves;
And o'er its head a skylark's voice
   Consoles the spirits of the slaves.

                      R. H. HORNE.

THE CHESTNUT-TREE.

WITHIN the green heart of a wood
  A stately chestnut-tree once stood;
Its great trunk, straight and high,
And mighty branches, stretching wide,
Around, about, on every side,
  Seemed reaching to the sky.

When spring-time came, and soft winds blew,
Its leafy blossoms then burst through
  Their wintry prison-cells;
And through the long, sweet summer days
Were heard from it the wild, sweet lays
  That from a bird's throat swells.

And summer passed, and autumn came,
And all the forest seemed aflame
  With dyes of red and gold.
When trees their brightest raiment wore,
The stately chestnut-tree then bore
  A wealth of nuts untold.

But through the changes of the year,
From budding spring to winter drear,
  None saw the chestnut-tree;
Unknown, unnoted, day by day,
Though seasons came and passed away,
  It lived contentedly.

And though no happy children played
Beneath its branches' grateful shade,
  Or came with laughter gay,

When lingering summer cast its fair,
Sweet, hazy spell on autumn's air,
　To carry nuts away.

Yet still the tree grew fair and strong;
Its every rustling was a song
　Of praise to God on high.
What though its nuts unheeded fell?
They served the small gray squirrel well,
　Who made his home near by.

And thus the tree its course lived through
Although no good it seemed to do,
　Such useless life it led.
But who can say that mighty tree
Fulfilled not its true destiny
　When it a squirrel fed?

　　　　　　　　　　JANE CAMPBELL.

A GARDEN SCENE.

WHAT wondrous life is this I lead?
　　Ripe apples drop about my head;
The luscious clusters of the vine
Upon my mouth do crust their wine.
The nectarine, and curious peach,
Into my hands themselves do reach.
Stumbling on melons, as I pass,
Ensnared with flowers, I fall on grass.
Meanwhile the mind from pleasures less
Withdraws into its happiness.

The mind, that ocean, where each kind
Does straight its own resemblance find;
Yet it creates, transcending these,
Far other worlds, and other seas,
Annihilating all that's made
To a green thought in a green shade.
Here at the fountain's shaded foot,
Or at some fruit-tree's mossy root,
Casting the body's vest aside,
My soul into the boughs does glide;
There, like a bird, it sits and sings,
Then wets and claps its silver wings,
And, till prepared for longer flight,
Waves in its plumes the various light.
How well the skillful gardener drew,
Of flowers and herbs, this dial new,
Where, from above, the milder sun
Does through a fragrant zodiac run;
And, as it works, the industrious bee
Computes its time as well as we.
How could such sweet and wholesome hours
Be reckoned, but with herbs and flowers?

MARVELL.

LIBERTY TREE.

Published in 1775.

IN a chariot of light from the regions of day
    The Goddess of Liberty came;
Ten thousand celestials directed the way,
    And hither conducted the dame.

A fair, budding branch from the gardens above,
  Where millions with millions agree,
She brought in her hand, as a pledge of her love,
  And the plant she named Liberty Tree.

The celestial exotic struck deep in the ground,
  Like a native it flourished and bore;
The fame of its fruit drew the nations around,
  To seek out this peaceable shore.
Unmindful of names or distinctions they came,
  For freemen like brothers agree;
With one spirit endued, they one friendship pursued,
  And their temple was Liberty Tree.

Beneath this fair tree, like the patriarchs of old,
  Their bread in contentment they ate;
Unvexed with the troubles of silver and gold,
  The cares of the grand and the great.
With timber and tar they old England supplied,
  And supported her power on the sea;
Her battles they fought, without getting a groat,
  For the honor of Liberty Tree.

But hear, O ye swains, 'tis a tale most profane,
  How all the tyrannical powers,
Kings, commons, and lords, all uniting amain,
  Strove to cut down this guardian of ours;
From the east to the west sounded the trumpet, "To arms!"
  Through the broad land they bade the sound flee,
Bade the far and the near all unite with a cheer,
  In defense of our Liberty Tree.

WILD FLOWERS.

SCATTERED over glade and dingle,
   Freshly bathed in balmy showers,
Where the lights and shadows mingle,
   Children find a wealth of flowers.

Roots, that careful hands have planted,
   May not feel the sun and air;
Though ye watch, by hope enchanted,
   Still your garden soil is bare.

Yet the ivy fetters lightly
   Rugged tree and ruined wall;
And upon the wayside brightly
   Snows of scented hawthorn fall.

Kingcups in their golden glory,
   Daisies on the churchyard sod,
Tell the world's unwritten story;
   Silent witnesses of God.

In our life's deserted places
   Flowers, by human hands unsown,
Blossom with a thousand graces
   Making every spot their own.

Unexpected joys are springing
   In the paths we feared to tread;
Love, with tender fibres clinging,
   Clasps the hope we counted dead.

Gifts, for which we have not striven,
  On our darkest hours descend;
Blessings by a Father given,
  Strew the pathway to the end.

     SARAH DOUDNEY.

THE TREE.

I LOVE thee when thy swelling buds appear
  And one by one their tender leaves unfold,
As if they knew that warmer suns were near,
  Nor longer sought to hide from winter's cold:
And when with darker growth thy leaves are seen,
  To veil from view the early robin's nest,
I love to lie beneath thy waving screen
  With limbs by summer's heat and toil oppressed;
And when the autumn winds have stripped thee bare,
  And round thee lies the smooth, untrodden snow,
When naught is thine that made thee once so fair,
  I love to watch thy shadowy form below,
And through thy leafless arms to look above
On stars that brighter beam, when most we need
  their love.

     JONES VERY.

DECORATION DAY

THE SOLDIER'S TENT.

Translated by Carmen Sylva.

ACROSS the mountains the mist hath drawn
   A cov'ring of bridal white;
The plains afar make lament, and mourn
That the flutt'ring veil of the mist-wreaths born
   Hath hidden the mountains from sight.

The soldier lay smiling peacefully
   Asleep in his tent on the sward,
The moon crept in and said: "Look at me,
A glance from thy sweetheart am I, for thee!"
   But he answered: "I have my sword."

Then the rustling wind drew softly near,
   Played round him with whispers light:
"I am the sighs of thy mother dear,
The sighs of thy mother am I, dost hear?"
   But he answered: "I have the fight."

Then night sank down from the dark'ning sky
   Round the sleeper, and murmured: "Rest,
Thy sweetheart's veil o'er thy face doth lie!"
But he answered: "No need of it have I,
   For the banner doth cover me best."

By his tent the river, clear and wide,
  Rolled onward its silver flood,
And said: "I am water, the cleansing tide,
More blessèd than aught in the world beside."
  But he answered: "I have my blood."

Then Sleep drew near to his tent, and low
  She whispered with soothing breath:
'I am Sleep, the healer of ev'ry woe,
The dearest treasure of man below."
  But the soldier replied: "I have Death."

Across the mountains the mist hath drawn
  A cov'ring of bridal white;
The plains afar make lament, and mourn
That the flutt'ring veil of the mist-wreaths born,
  Hath hidden the mountains from sight.
HÉLÉNE VACARESCO.

DECORATION DAY.

YES, scatter flowers above the graves
  Where the Nation's dead are sleeping,
To tell that the comrades left behind
  Their memories green are keeping.

'Tis many a year since they marched forth,
  All the battle's perils braving,
And many a year above their graves
  Has the long green grass been waving.

Yes, scatter the flowers, 'tis a kindly thought,
   Pale lilies and fair red roses,
With lavish hands o'er the grave where each
   Brave soldier in peace reposes.
Long years have passed since they sank to rest,
   'Mid a nation's bitter mourning,
But their faithful comrades, year by year,
   Bring flowers for their graves' adorning.

But far away upon hill and plain,
   Nameless, forgotten, are lying,
The bones of many who bravely fought,
   In their country's service dying.
But though their graves are unknown, unsought,
   Our dear Lord covers them over
With the sweetest flowers and greenest grass,
   And blossoms of scented clover.

And instead of the muffled beat of drums,
   Its saddening memories bringing,
The on'y sound that the silence breaks
   Is the note of some wild bird singing,
Or a rush of timid, rapid feet
   As the wild gray rabbit passes,
Or the drowsy hum of the honey-bee
   As it flits among the grasses.

But peacefully still at rest they lie
   And little it matters whether,
Alone they sleep in their nameless graves,
   Or in churchyards close together.

For a grateful country in its heart
  Is fresh their memories keeping.
So scatter flowers with a generous hand
  Where the Nation's dead are sleeping.

JANE CAMPBELL.

THE DEAD TRUMPETER.

WAKE, soldier! wake! thy war-horse waits,
  To bear thee to the battle back;
Thou slumberest at the foeman's gates;
  The dog would break thy bivouac;
Thy plume is trailing in the dust,
And thy red falchion gathering rust!

Sleep, soldier! sleep! thy warfare o'er,
  Not thine own bugle's loudest strain
Shall ever break thy slumbers more,
  With summons to the battle plain;
A trumpet-note more loud and deep
Must rouse thee from that leaden sleep!

Thou need'st not helm nor cuirass now,
  Beyond the Grecian hero's boast,—
Thou wilt not quail thy naked brow,
  Nor shrink before a myriad host,—
For head and heel alike are sound,
A thousand arrows cannot wound.

Thy mother is not in thy dreams,
  With that wild widowed look she wore

The day- -how long to her it seems!—
  She kissed thee at the cottage door,
And sickened at the sounds of joy
That bore away her only boy!

Sleep, soldier!—let thy mother wait
  To hear thy bugle on the blast;
Thy dog, perhaps, may find the gate,
  And bid her home to thee at last;
He cannot tell a sadder tale
Than did thy clarion on the gale,
    When last—and far away—she heard
Its lingering echoes fail.

T. K. HERVEY.

THE DEAD VOLUNTEER.

SILENTLY, tenderly, mournfully home,
  From the red battlefield volunteers come—
    Not with a loud hurrah,
    Not with a wild *éclat*,
    Not with the tramp of war,
    Come our brave sons from far.
Gently and noiselessly bear him along;
Hushed be the battle-cry, music, and song.

Silently, tenderly, mournfully home,
Not as they marched away, volunteers come—
    Not with the sword and gun,
    Not with the stirring drum,
    Come our dead heroes home.
    Now all his work is done,

Thoughtfully, prayerfully bear ye the dead,
Pillow it softly—the volunteer's head.

Silently, tenderly, mournfully home,
Where should the brave volunteer come,
    But to his native hills,
     Where the bright gushing rills,
     Freedom's sweet music fills,
     And her soft dew distills?
Peacefully, prayerfully lay our brave friend
Close to the home he fought to defend.

Silently, tearfully welcome the brave,—
Glory encircles the patriot's grave.
    Here let affection swell,
    Here let the marble tell
    How the brave hero fell,
    Loving his country well.
Silently, tenderly, mournfully home,
Welcome the brave volunteers as they come.

                J. W. BARKER.

THE FALLEN.

TOLL the slow bell,
  Toll the low bell,
    Toll, toll,
    Make dole
For them that wrought so well;
To them that fought and fell,

Once more, farewell. farewell,
Once more, farewell.

Come, come,
Bid the dull **drum**
Hush gladness dumb,
Let dolorous horn, and drum, **and bell**
The steady voice of sorrow swell.
Solemn measures slow
Toll, and beat, and blow;
Rebuke it, darken, blight
This bright, unpitying light;
Put out all glories that adorn
This sweet, unheeding morn.
      Toll—toll—
      Toll—toll—
For them, our beauty and our might,
Gone on the unreturning way,
For them that took the night
That we might have the day.

Blow the sad horn
This glad May morn;
Knell, knell,
Let the slow bell
Be struck, and the troubled **drum.**
Come, come,
Blow the sad horns,
Bring flowers for them that took the **thorns.**

The sacred scroll—let it once more be read;
Victors and vanquished, all the fallen together.

Remember all; here in the warm, May weather,
Number once more the well-belovéd dead.
Love forgets no brother
Born of our common mother;
Here in the warm May weather,
Bow we in grief together;
To them that fought so well,
To all that fought and fell,
Once more, farewell, farewell,
Once more, farewell.

Death, Death!
At whose breath,
By whose will, is he?
Oh! if Death could be,
These would he find foremost among his foes,
These who, though now they tent
Beyond the firmament,
Deliver still their undiminished blows;
Who, marching bright and far
As flames the farthest star,
Along the fadeless fields of light,
The ringing field of life and right,
Forever gather to the fight.

No more let Grief with his pale face
Offend the splendor and the grace,
The promise, of this place.
Bid hither cringing Doubt,
And drive his devil out:
The Lord our God, once more He saith,—
"This hand made all; it made not Death."

Sepulchred not, but sown
In virtuous mold, the hardy seed
For harvest of th' enduring deed,
Here live and thrive God's own.
Here did our soldiers, one by one,—
The last grand duty grandly done,—
These acres of green martyr sward
Add to the garden of our Lord.
Live words, swift words, and joyous, break
From these still mounds:—
Wake, Freedom, wake!"
Blow the glad horn
This bright May morn,
This white May morn;
Strike up the martial stave;
Say, where those colors wave
Believed and battled they
Whose face was toward the day;
Say, there no cowl nor crown
Strike Freedom down;
Say on till Hell itself shall hear,
Men are that falter not nor fear;
Say, for the brave
" There is no grave."

Ay, come, come,
Strike the quick drum,
Smite sorrow dumb.
Staunch, undaunted measures blow,
Gath'ring courage as they go:
Again and yet again say for this land,

Her soldier's sword is firm in his good hand,
Say, these fix yet
The bayonet,
And stiff the thrust
Up through the dust,—
Far as yon sovran colors wave,
Blow, blow their challenge to the grave.

     JOHN VANCE CHENEY.

HIS MOTHER'S SONG.

BENEATH the hot midsummer sun,
 The men had marched all day;
And now beside a rippling stream,
 Upon the grass they lay.
Tiring of games and idle jest
 As swept the hours along,
They cried to one who mused apart:
 "Come, friend, give us a song."

"I fear I cannot please," he said;
 "The only songs I know
Are those my mother used to sing
 For me long years ago."
"Sing one of those," a rough voice cried,
 "There's none but true men here;
To every mother's son of us
 A mother's songs are dear."

Then sweetly rose the singer's voice
    Amid unwonted calm;
"'Am I a soldier of the cross,
    A follower of the Lamb?
And shall I fear to own His cause?'"
    The very stream was stilled,
And hearts that never throbbed with fear
    With tender thoughts were filled

Ended the song; the singer said,
    As to his feet he rose,
"Thanks to you all, my friends, good-night,
    God grant us sweet respose."
"Sing us one more," the captain begged,
    The soldier bent his head,
Then glancing round with smiling lips,
    "You'll join with me?" he said.

"We'll sing the old familiar air,
    Sweet as the bugle-call,
'All hail the power of Jesus' name,
    Let angels prostrate fall.'"
Ah! wondrous was the old tune's spell,
    As on the soldier sang,
Each eye was moist with mem'ry's tear,
    And loud the voices rang.

The songs are done, the camp is still,
    Naught but the stream is heard;
But ah! the depths of every soul
    By those old hymns are stirred.

And up from many a bearded lip
   In whispers soft and low,
Rises the prayer mother taught
   Her boy long years ago.

THE VOLUNTEER.

"At dawn," he said, " I bid them all farewell,
   To go where bugles call and rifles gleam."
And with the restless thought asleep he fell,
   And glided into dream.

A great hot plain from sea to mountain spread,
   Through it a level river slowly drawn;
He moved with a vast crowd, and at its head
   Streamed banners like the dawn.

There came a blinding flash, a deafening roar,
   And dissonant cries of triumph and dismay;
Blood trickled down the river's reedy shore,
   And with the dead he lay.

The morn broke in upon his solemn dream,
   And still, with steady pulse and deepening eye,
"Where bugles call," he said, "and rifles gleam,
   I follow, though I die."

ELBRIDGE JEFFERSON CUTLER.

THE DEAD COMRADE.

At the burial of Grant, a bugler stood forth and sounded " Taps."

COME, soldiers, arouse ye!
   Another has gone;
Let us bury our comrade,
   His battles are done.
His sun it is set;
   He was true, he was brave,
   He feared not the grave,
There is naught to regret.

Bring music and banners
   And wreaths for his bier,—
No fault of the fighter
   That Death conquered here.
Bring him home ne'er to rove,
   Bear him home to his rest,
   And over his breast
Fold the flag of his love.

Great Captain of battles,
   We leave him with Thee!
What was wrong, O forgive it;
   His spirit make free.
Sound taps, and away!
   Out lights, and to bed!
   Farewell, soldier dead!
Farewell—for a day.

                  RICHARD WATSON GILDER.

MEMORIAL DAY.

THE circling year again brings **round**
   This proud Memorial Day,
With mingled joy and grief profound,
We deck with wreaths the sacred **mound**,
   Where patriot soldiers lay.

'Tis meet that we this honor **show**,
   And pledge this day anew,
Our fadeless faith, that all may **know**
How strong this faith will ever **grow**,
   In loyal hearts and true.

Our land so broad, so grand, so **free**,
   Pays homage to the band,
Who fought and bled, and died **that we**
An undivided nation be,
   The peer of any land.

Pile granite to the vaulted **skies**;
   Carve words of deathless fame;
Let marble monuments arise
Where'er the soldier-patriot **lies**,
   In honor of his name.

The granite pile may sink to **dust**,
   No more its words be read;
The marble may forsake its trust;
The nation may, in reckless **lust**,
   Forget the honored dead.

Their fame is fixed beyond the skies,
  Their glory is of God;
'Twas not ambition's sacrifice,
Nor eager gain for worldly prize,
  That laid them 'neath the sod.

They died our nation's life to save,
  Ere it were rent in twain,
For this each fills a soldier's grave,
For this the glorious flag shall wave,
  In honor of the slain.

They died: the clanking shackles fell
  From bondman's fettered hand,
And angels winged their way to tell,
While heavenly choirs the anthem swell,
  Of freedom's happy land.

Z. F. Riley

FOURTH OF JULY

FREE AMERICA.

THAT seat of science, Athens,
   And earth's proud mistress, Rome;
Where now are all their glories?
   We scarce can find a tomb.
Then guard your rights, Americans,
   Nor stoop to lawless sway;
Huzza! then shout huzza! huzza
   For free America.

We led fair Freedom hither,
   And lo, the desert smiled!
A paradise of pleasure
   Was captured in the wild!
Your harvest, bold Americans,
   No power shall snatch away!
Then huzza! huzza! a loud huzza,
   For free America.

Torn from a land of tyrants,
   Beneath this western sky,
We formed a new dominion,
   A land of liberty;
The world shall own we're masters here;
   Then hasten on the day,

When every voice shall shout huzza
  For free America.

Proud Albion bowed to Cæsar,
  And numerous lords before;
To Picts, to Danes, to Normans,
  And many masters more:
But we can boast, Americans,
  We've never fallen a prey;
Then loud huzza! we'll sing huzza
  For free America!

We pray God bless our happy land,
  And through its vast domain
May hosts of heroes cluster,
  Who scorn to wear a chain;
And cursed be the fawning sycophant
  That dares our rights betray.
Huzza! huzza! boys; a loud huzza
  For our America.

Lift up your hands, ye heroes,
  And swear with proud disdain,
The traitor that would betray you
  Shall lay his snares in vain.
Should foreign foes spend all their force,
  We'll greater strength display,
Then shout huzza! huzza! huzza
  For our America.

And the future shall all hail us
  The masters of the main,

Our fleets shall speak in thunder;
   Hear it, England, France, and Spain
And the nations over the ocean spread
   Shall tremble and obey
The sons, the sons, the sons, the sons
   Of brave America.

OUR OWN DEAR LAND.

OUR own dear land, our native land,
   Home of the brave and free!
In vain we search old ocean's strand
   To find a land like thee.
Thy towering hills, thy prairies wide,
   Thy forests old and dim,
Thy streams that roll in matchless pride,
   Thy torrent's thunder-hymn.

Our own dear land, our native land,
   None can compare with thee;
The fairest work of nature's hand—
   Our own dear land for me!
Our own dear land, our native land,
   Fearless thy banner waves,
And nations yet unborn shall stand
   Beside thy heroes' graves.

Our fathers spurned oppression's laws,
   All fought for God and right;
So may their sons, in Freedom's cause,
   Be foremost in the fight!

Our own dear land, our native land,
　Home of the brave and free;
The finest work of nature's hand—
　Our own dear land for me!

J. R. THOMAS.

THE NATIONAL FLAG.

THERE is the national flag. He must be cold, indeed, who can look upon its folds rippling in the breeze without pride of country. If he be in a foreign land, the flag is companionship and country itself with all its endearments. Who, as he sees it, can think of a State merely? Whose eyes, once fastened upon its radiant trophies, can fail to recognize the image of the whole nation? It has been called a "floating piece of poetry," and yet I know not if it have an intrinsic beauty beyond other ensigns. Its highest beauty is in what it symbolizes. It is because of what it represents that all gaze at it with delight and reverence. It is a piece of bunting lifted in the air, but it speaks sublimely, and every part has a voice. Its stripes of alternate red and white proclaim the original union of thirteen States to maintain the Declaration of Independence. Its stars of white on a field of blue proclaim that union of States constituting our national constellation, which receives a new star with every new State. The two together signify union, past and present. The very colors have a language which was officially recognized by our fathers. White is for purity, red for valor, blue for justice; and all together, bunting, stripes, stars, and colors blazing in the sky, make the flag of our country—to be cherished by all our hearts, to be upheld by all our hands.

CHARLES SUMNER.

INDEPENDENCE DAY—1798.

SQUEAK the fife and beat the drum,
Independence Day has come!
Quickly rub the pewter platter,
Heap the nut-cakes fried in butter.
Set the cups, and beaker-glass,
The pumpkin and the apple-sauce;
Sambo play and dance with quality;
This is the day of blest equality.
Father and mother are but men,
And Sambo—is a citizen.
Now saw as fast as e'er you can do,
And father, you cross o'er to Sambo.
Thus we dance, and thus we play,
On glorious Independence Day.
Rub your rosin on your bow,
And let us have another go.
Zounds! As sure as eggs and bacon,
Here's Ensign Sneak and Uncle Deacon,
Aunt Thiah, and Cousin Bet behind her,
On blundering mare, than beetle blinder.
And there's the 'Squire, too, with his lady,

Dick, hold the beast, I'll take the baby.
Moll, bring the 'Squire our great arm-chair;
Good folks, we're glad to see you here.
*   *   *   *   *   *   *
Thus we dance and dance away,
This glorious INDEPENDENCE DAY!

ROYALL TYLER.

ADVICE TO MY COUNTRY.

AS this advice, if it ever see the light, will not do so till I am no more, it may be considered as issuing from the tomb, where truth alone can be respected, and the happiness of man alone consulted. It will be entitled, therefore, to whatever weight can be derived from good intentions, and from the experience of one who has served his country in various stations through a period of forty years; who espoused in his youth, and adhered through his life, to the cause of its liberty; and who has borne a part in most of the great transactions which will constitute epochs of its destiny.

The advice nearest to my heart and deepest in my convictions is: That the Union of the States be cherished and perpetuated. Let the open enemy to it be regarded as a Pandora with her box opened, and the disguised one as the serpent creeping with his deadly wiles into Paradise.

JAMES MADISON.

THE FIGHT.

TUGGED the patient, panting horses, as the colter,
    keen and thorough,
By the careful farmer guided, cut the deep and even
    furrow;
Soon the mellow mold in ridges, straightly pointed
    as an arrow,
Lay to wait the bitter vexing of the fierce, remorse
    less harrow;
Lay impatient for the seeding, for the growing and
    the reaping,
All the richer and the readier for the quiet winter
    sleeping.

At his loom the pallid weaver, with his feet upon the
    treadles,
Watched the threads alternate rising, with the lifting
    of the heddles.
Not admiring that, so swiftly, at his eager fingers
    urging,
Flew the bobbin-loaded shuttle 'twixt the filaments
    diverging,
Only labor, dull and cheerless, in the work before
    him seeing,
As the warp and woof uniting brought the figures
    into being.

Roared the fire before the bellows; glowed the forge's
    dazzling crater;

Rang the hammer on the anvil, both the lesser an
    the greater;
Fell the sparks around the smithy, keeping rhythm
    to the clamor,
To the ponderous blows and clanging of each unre-
    lenting hammer;
While the diamonds of labor, from the curse of Adam
    borrowed,
Glittered in a crown of honor on each iron-beater'-
    brow.

Through the air there came a whisper, deepening
    quickly into thunder,
How the deed was done that morning that would
    rend the realm asunder;
How at Lexington the Briton mingled causeless
    crime with folly,
And a king endangered empire by an ill-considered
    volley.
Then each heart beat quick for vengeance, as the
    anger-stirring story
Told of brethren and of neighbors lying corses stiff
    and gory.

Stops the plough and sleeps the shuttle, stills the
    blacksmith's noisy hammer,
Come the farmer, smith, and weaver, with a wrath
    too deep for clamor;
But their fiercely purposed doing every glance they
    give avouches,
As they handle rusty fire-locks, powder-horns and
    bullet pouches,

As they hurry from the workshops, from the fields
and from the forges,
Venting curses deep and bitter on the latest of the
Georges.

* * * * * * * *

I was but a beardless stripling on that chilly April
morning,
When the church-bells, backward ringing, to the
minute-men gave warning;
But I seized my father's weapons—he was dead who
one time bore them—
And I swore to use them stoutly, or to never more
restore them;
Bade farewell to sister, mother, and to one than either
dearer,
Then departed, as the firing told of red-coats drawing
nearer.

On the Britons came from Concord—'twas a name of
mocking omen;
Concord never more existed 'twixt our people and
the foemen;
On they came in haste from Concord, where a few
had stood to fight them,
Where they failed to conquer Buttrick, who had
stormed the bridge, despite them;
On they came, the tools of tyrants, 'mid a people who
abhorred them;
They had done their master's bidding, and we purposed to reward them.

'Twas a goodly sight to see them, but we heeded not
    its splendor,
For we felt their martial bearing hate within our
    hearts engender,
Kindling fire within our spirits, though our eyes a
    moment watered,
As we thought on Moore and Hadley, and their brave
    companions slaughtered;
And we swore to deadly vengeance for the fallen to
    devote them,
And our rage grew hotter, hotter, as our well-aimed
    bullets smote them.

When to Hardy's Hill their weary, waxing-fainter
    footsteps brought them,
There again the stout Provincials brought the wolves
    to bay and fought them;
And though often backward beaten, still returned the
    foe to follow,
Making forts of every hill-top, and redoubts of every
    hollow.
Hunters came from every farm-house, joining eagerly
    to chase them—
They had boasted far too often that we ne'er would
    dare to face them.

* * * * * * * *

With nine hundred came Lord Percy, sent by startled
    Gage to meet them,
And he scoffed at those who suffered such a horde of
    boors to beat them.

But his scorn was changed to anger, when on front
 and flank were falling
From the fences, walls, and roadsides drifts of leaden
 hail appalling;
And his picked and chosen soldiers, who had never
 shrunk in battle,
Hurried quicker in their panic when they heard the
 firelocks rattle.

Tell it not in Gath, Lord Percy, never Ascalon let
 hear it,
That you fled from those you taunted as devoid of
 force and spirit;
That the blacksmith, weaver, farmer, leaving forging,
 weaving, tillage,
Fully paid with coin of bullets base marauders for
 their pillage;
They, you said, would fly in terror, Britons and their
 bayonets shunning;
The loudest of the boasters proved the foremost in
 the running.

* * * * * * * *

Into Boston marched their forces, musket-barrels
 brightly gleaming,
Colors flying, sabres flashing, drums were beating,
 fifes were screaming.
Not a word about their journey; from the general to
 the drummer.
Did you ask about their doings, than a statue each
 was dumber;

But the wounded in their litters, lying pallid, weak, and gory,
With a language clear and certain, told the sanguinary story.

* * * * * * * *

On the day the fight that followed, neighbor met and talked with neighbor;
First the few who fell they buried, then returned to daily labor.
Glowed the fire within the forges, ran the ploughshare down the furrow,
Clicked the bobbin-shuttle—both our fight and toil was thorough;
If we labored in the battle, or the shop, or forge, or fallow,
Still came an honest purpose, casting round our deeds a halo.

Though they strove again, these minions of Germaine and North and Gower,
They could never make the weakest of our band before them cower;
Neither England's bribes nor soldiers, force of arms, nor titles splendid,
Could deprive of what our fathers left as right to be defended.
And the flame from Concord spreading, kindled kindred conflagrations,
Till the Colonies United took their place among the nations.

THOMAS DUNN ENGLISH.

OUR LAND.

THE sun shines not upon, has never shone upon a land where human happiness is so widely disseminated, where human government is so little abused, so free from oppression, so invisible, intangible, and yet so strong. Nowhere else do the institutions which constitute a State rest upon so broad a base as here, and nowhere are men so powerless and institutions so strong. In the wilderness of free minds dissensions will occur, and in the unlimited discussion in writing and in speech, in town meetings, newspapers, and legislative bodies, angry and menacing language will be used, irritations will arise and be aggravated, and those immediately concerned in the strife, or breathing its atmosphere, may fear, or feign to fear that danger is in such hot breath and passionate resolves. But outside, and above, and beyond all this are the people, steady, industrious, self-possessed, caring little for abstractions and less for abstractionists, but with one deep, common sentiment, and with the consciousness, calm, but quite sure and earnest, that in the Constitution and the Union, as they received them from their fathers, and as they themselves have observed and maintained them, is the sheet-anchor of their hope, the pledge of their prosperity, the palladium of their liberty; and with this is that other consciousness, not less calm and not less earnest, that in their own keeping exclusively, and not in that of any party leaders, or

party demagogues, or political hacks, or speculators
is the integrity of that Union and that Constitution
It is in the strong arms and honest hearts of the great
masses, and these masses, though slow to move, are
irresistible when the time and the occasion for moving
come. KING.

THE FIGHTING PARSON.

IT was brave young Parson Webster,
 His father a parson before him,
And here in this town of Temple
 The people used to adore him;
And the minute-men from all quarters
 That morning had grounded their arms
'Round the meeting-house on the hilltop,
 Looking down on Temple farms.

Dear to the Puritan soldier
 The food which his meeting-house offered,
And especially dear the fine manna
 Which the young Temple minister proffered;
And believe as he might in his firelock,
 His bayonet, or his sword,
The minute-man's heart was hopeless
 If not filled with the strength of the Lord.

The minute-man ever and always
 Waited the signal of warning,
And he never dreamed in the evening
 Where his prayers would ascend the next morning;

And they even said that the parson
   Undoubtedly preached his best
When his musket stood in the pulpit
   Ready for use with the rest.

Sad was the minister's message,
   And many a heart beat faster,
And many a soft eye glistened,
   Whenever the voice of the pastor
Dwelt on the absent dear ones
   Who had followed their country's call
To the distant camp, or the battle,
   Or the frowning fortress-wall.

And now when near to " fifteenthly,"
   And the urchins thought of their nuncheon,
And into the half-curtained windows
   Hotter and hotter the sun shone,
And the redbreast dozed in the branches,
   And the crow on the pine tree's top,
And the squirrel was lost in his musings,
   The sermon came to a stop.

For sharp on the turnpike the clatter
   Of galloping hoofs resounded,
And the granite ring of the roadway
   Louder and louder sounded;
And now no longer the redbreast
   Was inclined to be dull that day,
And now no longer the sexton
   Slept in his usual way.

But all sprang up on the instant,
   And the widest of eyes grew wider,
While on towards the porch, like a tempest,
   Came sweeping the horse and its rider;
And now from the din of the hoof-beats
   A trumpet voice leapt out,
And, tingling to its rafters,
   The church was alive with the shout,—

"Burgoyne's at Ticonderoga:
   Would you have the old fort surrender?"
"No, no!" cried the parson; "New Hampshire
   Will send the last man to defend her!"
But before he could shoulder his musket
   A Tory sang up from below,
"I hear a great voice out of heaven, sir,
   Warning us not to go."

Quick from the pulpit descending,
   With the agile step of a lion,—
"The voice you hear is from hell, sir!"
   Replied the young servant of Zion.
And out through the open doorway,
   And on past the porch he strode,
And the congregation came after,
   And gathered beside the road.

Sadly enough the colonel,
   The minute-men all arraying,
From the dusty cocked hat of the rider
   Drew the lots for going or staying.

Then waving his hat as he took it,
  And putting the spurs to his mare,
The stranger rode off to New Ipswich
  In a cheering that rent the air.

Worse than the shock of battle,
  Now came the sad leave-taking,
And to mothers and maids and matrons
  The deepest of grief and heart-aching;
And far on the road through the mountains
  Whence the rider had just come,
They followed the minute-men marching
  To the sound of the fife and the drum.

Long dead have they been who sat there
  At that feast of things eternal—
Long dead the laymen, the deacons,
  The lawyer, the doctor, the colonel;
Long dead the youths and the maidens,
  And long on the graves of all
Have the summers and the winters
  Their leaves and their snows let fall.

But whenever I come to the churchyard,
  Where, by the side of the pastor,
They afterwards laid the colonel,
  His friend in success and disaster,
I see again on the Common
  The minute-men all in array,
And again I behold the departure,
  The pastor leading the way.

And I think of the scene when his comrades
  Brought back the young pastor, dying,
To his home in the house of the colonel;
  And how, on his death-bed lying,
He took the hand that was offered,
  And, gazing far into the night,
Whispered, "I die for my country—
  I have fought—I have fought the good fight."
                    HENRY AMES BLOOD.

THE STARS AND STRIPES.

THE drums are beat, the trumpets blow,
  The black-mouthed cannon bay the foe.
Dark, bristling o'er each murky height,
And all the field is whirled in fight.

The long life in the drowsy tent
Fades from me like a vision spent—
I stand upon the battle's marge,
And watch the smoking squadron's charge.

Behold one starry banner reel
With that wild shock of steel on steel;
And ringing up by rock and tree
At last the cry that summons me.

I hear it in my vibrant soul,
Deep thundering back its counter-roll;
And all life's ore seems newly wrought
In the white furnace of my thought.

No dream that made my dream divine,
But flashes back some mystic sign;
And every shape that erst was bright
Sweeps by me, garmented in light.

High legends of immortal praise,
Brows of world heroes bound with bays.
The crownèd majesties of Time
Rise visioned on my soul sublime.

Dear living lips of love and prayer
Sound chanting through the blackened air;
And eyes look out of marble tombs,
And hands are waved from churchyard gloom

"Charge! charge!"
We pant, we speed, we leap, we fly;
I feel my lifting feet aspire,
As I were born of wind and fire!

On! on! where wild the battle swims,
On! on! no shade my vision dims;
Transcendent o'er yon smoky wreath,
I see the glory of great death!

Come, flashing blade and hissing ball,
I give my blood, my breath, my all,
So that on yonder rocking height
The stars and stripes may wave to-night
LUCRETIA G. NOBLE.

THANKSGIVING DAY

JERICHO BOB.

JERICHO BOB, when he was four years old, hoped that one day he might be allowed to eat just as much turkey as he possibly could. He was eight now, but that hope had not been realized.

Mrs. Jericho Bob, his mother, kept hens for a living, and she expected that they would lay enough eggs in the course of time to help her son to an independent career as a bootblack.

They lived in a tumble-down house in a waste of land near the steam cars, and besides her hens Mrs. Bob owned a goat.

Our story has, however, nothing to do with the goat except to say he was there, and that he was on nibbling terms, not only with Jericho Bob, but with Bob's bosom friend, Julius Cæsar Fish, and it was surprising how many old hat-brims and other tidbits of clothing he could swallow during a day.

As Mrs. Bob truly said, it was no earthly use to

get something new for Jericho, even if she could afford it; for the goat browsed all over him, and had been known to carry away even a leg of his trousers.

Jericho Bob was eight years old, and the friend of his bosom, Julius Cæsar Fish, was nine. They were so much alike that if it hadn't been for Jericho's bow-legs and his turn-up nose, you really could not have told them apart.

A kindred taste for turkey also united them.

In honor of Thanksgiving day Mrs. Bob always sacrificed a hen which would, but for such blessed release, have died of old age. One drumstick was given to Jericho, whose interior remained an unsatisfied void.

Jericho Bob had heard of turkey as a fowl larger, sweeter, and more tender than hen; and about Thanksgiving time he would linger around the provision stores and gaze with open mouth at the noble array of turkeys hanging head downward over bushels of cranberries, as if even at that uncooked stage, they were destined for one another. And turkey was his dream.

It was spring-time, and the hens were being a credit to themselves. The goat in the yard, tied to a stake, was varying a meal of old shoe and tomato-can by a nibble of fresh green grass. Mrs. Bob was laid up with rheumatism.

"Jericho Bob!" she said to her son, shaking her red and yellow turban at him, "Jericho Bob, you go down an' fetch de eggs to-day. Ef I find yer don't bring me twenty-three, I'll—well, never mind what I'll do, but yer won't like it."

Now, Jericho Bob meant to be honest, but the fact was he found twenty-four, and the twenty-fourth was so big, so remarkably big.

Twenty-three eggs he brought to Mrs. Bob, but the twenty-fourth he sinfully left in charge of the discreet hen.

On his return he met Julius Cæsar Fish, with his hands in his pockets and his head extinguished by his grandfather's fur cap.

Together they went toward the hen-coop, and Julius Cæsar Fish spoke, or rather lisped (he had lost some of his front teeth):

"Jericho Bobth, tha'th a turkey'th egg."

"Yer don't say so?"

"I think i'th a-goin' ter hatch." No sooner said than they heard a pick and a peck in the shell.

"Pick!" a tiny beak broke through the shell. "Peck!" more beak. "Crack!" a funny little head, a long, bare neck, and then "Pick! peck! crack!" before them stood the funniest, fluffiest brown ball resting on two weak little legs.

"Hooray!" shouted the woolly heads.

"Peep!" said turkeykin.

"It's mine!" Jericho shouted excitedly.

"I'th Marm Pitkin'th turkey'th; she laid it there."

"It's mine, and I'm going to keep it, and next Thanksgiving I'm going ter eat him."

"Think your ma'll let you feed him up for thath?" Julius Cæsar asked, triumphantly.

Jericho Bob's next Thanksgiving dinner seemed destined to be a dream. His face fell.

"I'll tell yer whath I'll do," his friend said, benevolently; "I'll keep'm for you, and Thanksgivin we'll go halvth."

Jericho resigned himself to the inevitable, and the infant turkey was borne home by his friend.

Fish, Jr., lived next door, and the only difference in the premises was a freight-car permanently switched off before the broken-down fence of the Fish yard; and in this car turkeykin took up his abode.

I will not tell you how he grew and more than realized the hopes of his foster-fathers, nor with what impatience and anticipation they saw spring, summer, and autumn pass, while they watched their Thanksgiving dinner stalk proudly up the bare yard and even hop across the railroad tracks.

But, alas! the possession of the turkey brought with it strife and discord.

Quarrels arose between the friends as to the prospective disposal of his remains. We grieve to say that the question of who was to cook him led to blows.

It was the day before Thanksgiving. There was a coldness between the friends which was not dispelled by the bringing of a pint of cranberries to the common store by Jericho, and the contributing thereto of a couple of cold-boiled sweet potatoes by Julius Cæsar Fish.

The friends sat on an ancient wash-tub in the back

yard, and there was a momentary truce between them. Before them stood the freight-car, and along the track beyond an occasional train tore down the road, which so far excited their mutual sympathy that they rose and shouted as one man.

At the open door of the freight-car stood the unsuspecting turkey and looked meditatively out on the landscape and at the two figures on the wash-tub.

One had bow-legs, a turn-up nose, and a huge straw hat. The other wore a fur cap and a gentleman's swallow-tail coat, with the tails caught up because they were too long.

The turkey hopped out of the car and gazed confidingly at his protectors. In point of size he was altogether their superior.

"I think," said Jericho Bob, "we'd better ketch 'im. To-morrow's Thanksgiving. Yum!"

And he looked with great joy at the innocent, the unsuspecting fowl.

"Butcher Tham 'th goin' ter kill 'im for uth," Julius Cæsar hastened to say, "an' I kin cook 'im."

"No, you aint. I'm goin' to cook 'im," Jericho Bob cried, resentfully. "He's mine."

"He ainth; he'th mine."

"He was my egg," and Jericho Bob danced defiance at his friend.

The turkey looked on with some surprise, and he became alarmed when he saw his foster-fathers clasped in an embrace more of anger than of love.

"I'll eat 'im all alone!" Jericho Bob cried

"No, yer sha'n't!" the other shouted.

The turkey shrieked in terror and fled in a circle about the yard.

"Now, look yere," said Julius Cæsar, who had conquered, "we're goin' to be squar'. He wath your egg, but who brought 'im up? Me! Who'th got a friend to kill 'im? Me! Who'th got a fire to cook 'im? Me! Now you git up and we'll kitch 'im. Ef you thay another word about your egg I'll jeth eat 'im up all mythelf."

Jericho Bob was conquered. With mutual understanding they approached the turkey.

"Come yere; come yere," Julius Cæsar said, coaxingly.

For a moment the bird gazed at both, uncertain what to do.

"Come yere," Julius Cæsar repeated, and made a dive for him. The turkey spread his tail. Oh! didn't he run.

"Now I've got yer!" the wicked Jericho Bob cried, and thought he had captured the fowl, when with a shriek from Jericho Bob, as the turkey knocked him over, the Thanksgiving dinner spread his wings, rose in the air, and alighted on the roof of the freight-car.

The turkey looked down over the edge of the car at his enemies, and they gazed up at him. Both parties surveyed the situation.

"We've got him," Julius Cæsar cried at last, exultantly. "You git on the roof, and ef you don't kitch 'im up thar, I'll kitch 'im down yere."

With the help of the wash-tub, an old chair, Julius Cæsar's back, and much scrambling, Jericho

Bob was hoisted on top of the car. The turkey was stalking solemnly up and down the roof with tail and wings half spread.

"I've got yer now," Jericho Bob said, creeping softly after him. "I've got yer now, sure," he was just repeating, when with a deafening roar the express train for New York came tearing down the road.

For what possible reason it slowed up on approaching the freight-car nobody ever knew, but the fact remains that it did just as Jericho Bob laid his wicked black paw on the turkey's tail.

The turkey shrieked, spread his wings, shook the small black boy's grasp from his tail, and with a mighty swoop alighted on the roof of the very last car as it passed, and in a moment more Jericho Bob's Thanksgiving dinner had vanished, like a beautiful dream, down the road.

What became of that Thanksgiving dinner no one ever knew. If you happen to meet a traveling turkey without any luggage, but with a smile on his countenance. please send word to Jericho Bob.

ANNA EICHBERG KING.

DAISY'S THANKSGIVING.

NOW kitten-cat Daisy, just hear me,
  And 'tend to each word that I say,
And don't frisk around so 'bout nothing,
  To-morrow'll be Thanksgiving Day.

And if you don't chew up your ribbon,
  Nor dabble it round in the snow,
But behave all the time, just as pretty,
  You'll have something splendid, you know.

There's another thing, Daisy, I'll tell you,
  Aunt Mary is coming to-day,
To show us a sweet, darling baby
  That's named just like me—Allie May.
And if it should happen to squeeze you,
  Or pull your long tail the least mite,
You are not to scratch her nor bite her,
  For that wouldn't be just polite.

We must do all we can that'll please her,
  She being our company so;
Besides, such a new little baby
  Ain't had time to learn better, you know.
So if she does tease you, dear Daisy,
  Though, of course, I don't say it is right,
Please just get away from her easy,
  Not scratching the least little mite.

I s'pose you don't know 'bout Thanksgiving,
  'Cause you haven't had one before;
I'll tell you: there'll be a big turkey,
  And pie made of chickens,—and more.
And puddings all full of sweet raisins,
  And jelly and jam—such a treat!
And if you're a good kitten, Daisy,
  You'll get a plate full to eat.

MARGIE'S THANKSGIVING.

"With salt and potatoes and meal for bread,
  We needn't be hungry to-day," she said.
"Though I cannot stir from this queer old chair,
I look at the cupboard and know they're there;
And mother has left this lunch by me;
How thankful I am for it all," said she.

'With coal for the stove, and a quilt for the bed,
We needn't be chilly to-day," she said;
"For as long as my arms and back don't tire,
I can reach very well to feed the fire;
And mother 'll be home to an early tea;
How thankful I am for it all," said she.

"There's only one thing that I really dread,
And that is the pain in my back," she said;
"But it's better, a great deal better, I know.
Than it was at the first, three months ago;
And the doctor is ever so kind to me;
How thankful I am for it all," said she.

"And by and by, when the winter is dead,
He thinks I'll be almost well," she said;
"And I'll have some crutches and walk, and then
I can get the dinners for mother again;
And, oh! how glad and happy we'll be!
How thankful I am for it all," said she.

E. S. BUMSTEAD.

POLLY'S THANKSGIVING.

SUCH a funny little roly-poly Polly as she was, with her big china-blue eyes that were forever seeing something to wonder about, and her round, red cheeks that always grew redder when anybody spoke to her, and her crinkly flaxen hair that never would stay in place. Such a queer little dumpling of a Polly!

All the same, she liked nice things to eat as well as any one could, and when, once upon a time, somebody gave her the measles just in season for Thanksgiving Day, she felt dreadfully about it, and cried as hard as she knew how because she couldn't have any turkey, nor pudding, nor mince-pie for dinner—nothing at all but oatmeal gruel.

But crying didn't help the measles a mite, as of course Polly knew it wouldn't, but she couldn't have helped crying if she wanted to, and she didn't want to.

"'Most anybody'd cried, I wouldn't wonder," she said, a day or two after, when the measles had begun to go away again, "not to have a mite of any Thanksgiving for dinner, not any pie, not any cran'b'ry sauce, not any—O de-ar!"

"Well, well," said Polly's mother, laughing, "I guess we'll have to have another Thanksgiving Day right off."

"Oh! can we?" cried Polly, brightening up.

"Not without the governor says so," answered her father, with a twinkle. "The governor makes Thanksgiving Days, Polyanthus."

"Where does he live?" asked Polly, with an earnestness that was funny. Everybody laughed.

"At the capital," said Polly's Uncle Ben Davis. "Do you know where that is?"

"I guess I do," said Polly, and she asked no more questions.

But what do you guess this funny Polly did? By and by, when she felt quite like herself again, she borrowed pencil and paper and shut herself up in her own little room and wrote a letter that looked a little queer, 'tis true, but still made her wishes known.

"DeRe MisTeR GuvNeR will yOu PLeAse MAKE AnOTHeR THANKSGIVING DAy be caws I haD THE MEESLES the LAst One.

"POLLY PINKHAM."

Then she folded the letter and put it in an envelope, with one of her chromo cards, and sealed it, and took two cents out of her bank for the postage and ran away to the post-office as fast as she could run.

Mr. Willey kept the post-office, and if he himself had been behind the glass boxes that day, I don't believe Polly's letter ever would have gone out of Tinkerville. But Mr. Willey's niece was there. She read the address on the envelope Polly handed in, and her eyes danced. It looked so funny:

"Mister GuvNER, at the CAPITLE."

One or two questions brought out the whole story.

"The governor shall have your letter, Polly," roguish Miss Molly said, with a laugh, as she stamped it and wrote the postmark plain as plain could be.

And so he did. For, not quite a week later, a letter came in the mail to Polly—a great, white letter with a picture in one corner that made Polly's father open his eyes.

"Why, it's the State's arms," said he. "What under the sun—"

But I think he suspected. Oh! how red Polly's cheeks were, and how her small fingers trembled when she tore open her letter. It was printed so that she could read it herself, all but the long words.

"Dear Miss Polly:—Your letter received. I am very sorry you were so ill as not to be able to eat any Thanksgiving dinner. It was quite too bad. I hereby appoint a special Thanksgiving Day for you —next Thursday, December 9th—which I trust may be kept with due form.

"Your friend and well-wisher,
"Andrew Colburn."

"Oh! oh! oh!" cried Polly, hopping on one foot, "will you mother? O mother! will you? I wrote to him myself. Oh! I'm so glad."

"Did you ever!" cried Polly's mother. "Why, Polly Pinkham!" But Polly's father slapped his knee and laughed.

"Good for Governor Colburn! I'll vote for him

as long as he wants a vote. And Polly shall have a special Thanksgiving worth telling of, so she shall."

And so she did have, the very best she ever remembered.

A. C. STODDARD.

THANKSGIVING.

THANKS be to God! to whom earth owes
    Sunshine and breeze,
The heath-clad hill, the vale's repose,
    Streamlet and seas,
The snowdrop and the summer rose,
    The many-voicéd trees.

Thanks for the darkness that reveals
    Night's starry dower;
And for the sable cloud that heals
    Each fevered flower;
And for the rushing storm that peals
    Our weakness and Thy power.

Thanks for the sweetly-lingering might
    In music's tone;
For paths of knowledge, whose calm light
    Is all thine own;
For thoughts that at the Infinite
    Fold their bright wings alone.

Yet thanks that silence oft may flow
  In dewlike store:
Thanks for the mysteries that show
  How small our lore;
Thanks that we here so little know
  And trust Thee all the more!

Thanks for the gladness that entwines
  Our path below;
Each sunrise that incarnadines
  The cold, still snow;
Thanks for the light of love which shines
  With brightest earthly glow.

Thanks for Thine own thrice-blessed Word,
  And Sabbath rest;
Thanks for the hope of glory stored
  In mansions blest;
Thanks for the Spirit's comfort poured
  Into the trembling breast.

Thanks, more thanks, to Him ascend,
  Who died to win
Our life, and every trophy rend
  From Death and Sin;
Till, when the thanks of earth shall end,
  The thanks of Heaven begin.

      F. R. HAVERGAL.

THE TWILIGHT OF THANKSGIVING

THE day has lengthened into eve,
   And over all the meadows
The twilight's silent shuttles weave
   Their sombre web of shadows;
With northern lights the cloudless skies
   Are faintly phosphorescent,
And just above yon wooded rise
   The new moon shows her crescent.

Before the evening lamps are lit,
   While day and night commingle,
The sire and matron come and sit
   Beside the cozy ingle;
And softly speak of the delight
   Within their bosoms swelling,
Because beneath their roof to-night
   Their dear ones all are dwelling.

And when around the cheerful blaze
   The young folks take their places,
What blissful dreams of other days
   Light up their aged faces!
The past returns with all its joys,
   And they again are living
The years in which, as girls and boys,
   Their children kept Thanksgiving.

The stalwart son recalls the time
   When, urged to the endeavor,
He tried the well-greased pole to climb,
   And failed of fame forever.
The daughter tells of her emprise
   When, as a new beginner,
She helped her mother make the pies
   For the Thanksgiving dinner.

And thus with laugh and jest and song,
   And tender recollections,
Love speeds the happy hours along,
   And fosters fond affections;
While Fancy, listening to the mirth,
   And dreaming pleasant fictions,
Imagines through the winds on earth
   That heaven breathes benedictions.
WILLIAM D. KELLY